STUDENT UNIT GUIDE

NEW EDITION

Edexcel AS Economics Unit 1

Competitive Markets:
How They Work and Why They Fail

Mark Gavin

D1387184

PHILIP ALLAN

Philip Allan Updates, an imprint of Hodder Education, an Hachette UK company, Market Place, Deddington, Oxfordshire OX15 0SE

Orders
Bookpoint Ltd, 130 Milton Park, Abingdon, Oxfordshire, OX14 4SB
tel: 01235 827827
fax: 01235 400401
e-mail: education@bookpoint.co.uk
Lines are open 9.00 a.m.–5.00 p.m., Monday to Saturday, with a 24-hour message answering service. You can also order through the Philip Allan Updates website: www.philipallan.co.uk

ISBN 978-1-4441-4782-7

First printed 2011
Impression number   6
Year   2015   2014   2013

Printed in Dubai

Hachette UK's policy is to use papers that are natural, renewable and recyclable products and made from wood grown in sustainable forests. The logging and manufacturing processes are expected to conform to the environmental regulations of the country of origin.

P01922

Contents

Getting the most from this book

Questions & Answers

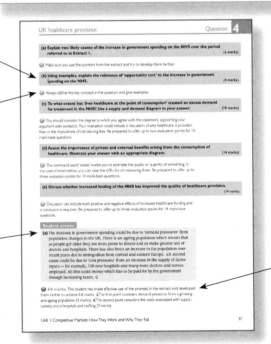

About this book

The aim of this guide is to help you prepare for the AS Unit 1 examination for economics 'Competitive markets – how they work and why they fail'. It should be used as a supplement for a taught course along with textbooks and other materials recommended by your teacher. There are two sections:

Content guidance — this summarises the specification content of AS Economics Unit 1. It is based on the price mechanism model which underpins the whole syllabus. It has been broken down into six topics and at the end of each there is a summary of key points.

Questions and answers – this provides guidance on how to answer supported multiple-choice and data-response questions. There are four sets of 'supported multiple-choice' questions with correct answers demonstrating maximum 4-mark responses. In addition, there are also four data-response questions with student answers and examiner comments on how to improve performance.

Content guidance

What is the nature of economics?

Economics can be defined as the allocation of scarce resources to provide for unlimited human wants.

Scarcity

Scarcity arises because there are insufficient resources to provide for everyone's wants. It occurs in all economies, since resources are finite compared to human material wants. Scarcity is obvious in countries that face famine or drought, where insufficient food or water is available to meet everyone's needs. However, scarcity also exists in wealthy countries, since not all human material wants can be satisfied.

Scarcity means we have to make choices over the use of our limited resources to provide for our material wants. Some crucial decisions have to be made over what, how and for whom to produce. These decisions face consumers, producers and the government. Once a decision has been made over what to use a resource for, opportunity cost arises.

Opportunity cost

Opportunity cost refers to the value of the next best alternative forgone. Consumers, producers and government all face opportunity cost.

A consumer may have £20 available to spend on a meal at a restaurant or on the next best thing, which is a new t-shirt. The individual cannot buy both at the same time. If the consumer chooses to buy a meal then the opportunity cost is forgoing the new t-shirt.

A firm may have £50,000 available to invest in a new machine or to invest in a training programme for employees. The managers have to make a choice over the best use of the funds.

A government may have an extra £100 million of tax revenue. It might use this to build a new hospital but in doing so, forgoes the building of a large school, considered to be the next best alternative.

Types of resources

Resources, or **factors of production**, are inputs used in the production of goods and services. They are finite and can be classified into four types: land, labour, capital and enterprise.

Knowledge check 1

What is the opportunity cost of you staying on at school or college to study A-levels?

Renewable and non-renewable resources

A **renewable resource** is one whose stock level can be maintained over a period of time. These include solar energy, wind power, water, oxygen, timber and soil. However, renewable resources may decline over time if they are consumed at a faster rate than the environment can replenish them. They require careful management, to avoid such things as deforestation and soil erosion.

A **non-renewable resource** is one whose stock level is decreased over time as it is consumed. These resources include fossil fuels such as coal, oil and gas. They also include commodities such as steel, copper and aluminium. It is possible to reduce the rate of decline of non-renewable resources through recycling and the development of substitutes. The price mechanism also has a role to play in reducing the rate of consumption via higher prices.

Production possibility frontiers

A **production possibility frontier** shows the maximum potential level of output for two goods or services that an economy can achieve when all its resources are fully and efficiently employed, given the level of technology available. It can be used to illustrate scarcity and opportunity cost.

Figure 1 shows the production possibility frontier of an economy with capital and consumer goods. Initially, the economy is at point *Z*. To increase the production of capital goods by 20 units and move to point *W*, there is an opportunity cost of 30 units of consumer goods.

Knowledge check 2

How might opportunity cost be shown on a production possibility frontier?

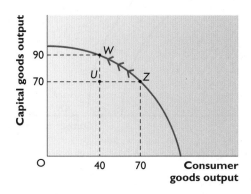

Figure 1 Production possibility frontier

The movement from *Z* to *W* increases the rate of economic growth, since capital goods are crucial for increasing production. Economic growth can be shown by an outward shift of the production possibility frontier. However, the loss of 30 units of consumer goods means that current living standards will fall in order to enable future living standards to rise at a faster rate.

If the economy is located at any point on its production possibility frontier, there is an efficient allocation of resources, since none are being wasted. However, if the economy is located within its production possibility frontier, there is an inefficient allocation of resources as not all are being used. At position *U* it is possible to increase

production of both consumer and capital goods, by utilising unemployed resources. Since nothing is given up in return, there is no opportunity cost.

The shape of production possibility frontiers — curves and straight lines

A typical production possibility frontier is bowed to the origin and shows that, as more of one good is produced, an increasing amount of the other good is forgone. The opportunity cost rises. This is because not all resources are as efficient as other resources in the production of both goods. Diminishing returns set in.

A good example is the use of agricultural land in East Anglia and southwest England. We can assume that farmland can be used either for growing wheat or for livestock production. East Anglia has highly fertile and light soils with suitable rainfall for growing wheat. Output per acre is very high. However, as we move towards the southwest, the soil becomes too heavy and rainfall too high for growing wheat. Instead, livestock farming is far more productive per acre. If farmland in the southwest was converted to wheat production, yields would be very low and at a cost of forgoing considerable livestock output.

Shifts in the production possibility frontier

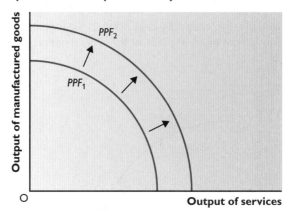

Figure 2 An increase in the production possibility frontier

A country's production potential may increase over time, which is shown in Figure 2 by an outward shift in its production possibility frontier. This represents economic growth and there are a number of possible causes: for example, an increase in the quantity or quality of resources; the expansion of further and higher education and government training schemes; or an increase in investment and development of new technology.

Occasionally the production possibility frontier may shift inwards towards the origin, indicating a decrease in the potential output of an economy. This may be caused by war or a natural disaster where many resources are destroyed. In 2011 an earthquake and the Tsunami it caused devastated coastal areas of Japan, reducing its productive capacity.

Examiner tip
Always define key economic concepts in the supported multiple-choice and data-response questions. Marks are always awarded for this.

Examiner tip
Be prepared to annotate or draw a diagram of a production possibility frontier when answering supported multiple-choice and data-response questions on this concept. Marks are usually available in the mark schemes.

Knowledge check 3
What is the state of the economy if it is operating at a point within its production possibility frontier?

Knowledge check 4
Outline the factors which might lead to an outward shift of the production possibility frontier for a country.

Specialisation and the division of labour

Specialisation occurs when an individual, a firm, a region or a country concentrates on the production of a limited range of goods and services. It has led to increases in productivity and living standards across the world. The UK specialises in the production of medicinal drugs, aircraft manufacture, tourism, and financial and business services. These goods and services can then be traded for other goods and services produced by other countries.

Specialisation can have disadvantages, notably when demand for a good or service falls, leading to a significant increase in unemployment. Also, a country specialising in the production and export of minerals may face problems of resource depletion.

The **division of labour** is one form of specialisation, where individuals concentrate on the production of a particular good or service. Production is broken down into a series of tasks, conducted by different workers. For example, house construction involves a range of specialist labour, including architects, surveyors, bricklayers, carpenters and electricians.

Advantages of the division of labour

- A person who spends time on one task quickly becomes highly skilled in it, e.g. a tyre fitter in a garage.
- No time is wasted in moving from one job to another, e.g. a packer on a sandwich production line.
- Capital equipment can be used continuously in production, e.g. the machinery on a motor vehicle production line.
- Less time is required to train workers for specific tasks.
- There is more choice of jobs for workers and they can specialise in tasks they are most suited to, e.g. a person who likes rock climbing might specialise in work as an outdoor pursuits leader.

These benefits lead to higher output per worker and thus help to reduce the cost per unit of output. Overall, living standards increase.

Disadvantages of the division of labour

- Repetition creates monotony and boredom. There could be a high turnover of staff, leading to increased recruitment and selection costs.
- Breaking down production into different tasks makes it easier to replace skilled workers with machines, leading to structural unemployment, e.g. motor vehicle welders being replaced by robots, or, supermarket cashiers being replaced with scanning machines.
- Specialisation creates interdependence in production. If one group of workers goes on strike, it could halt production across the whole industry. For example, when train drivers call a one-day stoppage, they disrupt the work of guards and ticket inspectors, as well as that of many commuters.

Examiner tip

Be careful not to confuse an increase in total production costs with a decrease in cost per unit of output. Specialisation will typically increase total production costs for a firm, since it is likely to increase total output, requiring more raw materials and machinery. However, it also leads to a reduction in the cost per unit of output, since workers become more productive.

Knowledge check 5

Why does the division of labour increase productivity or output per head?

Free-market and mixed economies

An economy can be organised in different ways to produce goods and services. This ranges along a continuum from a free-market economy through to a mixed economy and then a centrally planned economy. Figure 3 shows the notion of a continuum.

Percentage of resources allocated by the price mechanism

100%	50%	0%
Free-market economy All resources are allocated by the price mechanism. No government intervention.	**Mixed economy** Some resources are allocated by the price mechanism and some by the government.	**Centrally planned economy** All resources are allocated by the government. No price mechanism.

Figure 3 Types of economic system

In reality, the vast majority of economies comprise a mixture of both private enterprise (the private sector) and state intervention (the public sector), thus being mixed economies. In the UK around 60% of resources are allocated by the private sector and 40% by the public sector. The government is a major provider of education, healthcare, defence and law and order in society. In other European economies (e.g. France, Germany and Sweden), the size of the public sector is greater, while in North America (the USA and Canada) it is lower. In all cases these are considered to be mixed economies.

A free-market economy

This is an economy where decisions on what, how and for whom to produce are left to the operation of the price mechanism. Resources are privately owned and economic decision making is decentralised among many individual consumers and producers. There is minimum government intervention.

There are no pure free-market economies in the world today since, in every economy, the government directly controls some resources and output. However, the proportion of government intervention tends to be significantly less in some developing countries, such as Malaysia and Thailand, compared to the developed world. Perhaps the best example of a developed country with a relatively small government sector is Japan.

A mixed economy

This is an economy where decisions on what, how and for whom to produce are made partly by the private sector and partly by the government. Most developed countries in the world today fall under this classification. Examples are the UK, France, Germany, Canada, Australia and Sweden.

The rationale of a mixed economy is to gain the advantages of the market economy while avoiding its disadvantages through government intervention. Often government intervention occurs to correct market failure: for example, the under-provision of merit goods such as education and healthcare or the non-provision of public goods such as defence. Government intervention usually arises to help markets work more effectively.

Knowledge check 6

Which type of economic system best describes the UK?

A centrally planned economy (command economy)

This is an economy where the government makes the decisions on what, how and for whom to produce. In a command economy the government has control of resources and economic decision making is centralised. There is no role for the price mechanism. One example is North Korea.

Positive and normative economics

Positive economics

Positive economics is concerned with facts and is value-free. It is a scientific approach to the discipline, where economists explain the outcome of a particular policy, but are not expected to take sides. Positive statements can be tested as true or false by referring to the facts.

Normative economics

Normative economics is concerned with value-judgements and is a non-scientific approach to the discipline. A normative statement is an expression that something is right or wrong and so often includes the words *ought, should, fair, unfair, better* or *worse*.

Examiner tip
Use the term 'value-judgement' rather than 'opinion' when explaining a normative economic statement.

Examiner tip
Always use the information provided to explain why a statement is normative: for example, normative statements are often characterised by value-laden words such as *fair, unfair, better, worse, should* and *ought*.

Summary

- Economics is concerned with how resources are allocated to provide for human wants. As resources are finite, there is an opportunity cost in producing a good or service since the resources could have been used to produce alternative goods or services.

- The production possibility frontier illustrates the concepts of finite resources and opportunity cost. It can also be used to show unemployment and economic growth.

- Specialisation and the division of labour have led to huge increases in productivity.

- Most economies are mixed economies, where resources are allocated partly by private enterprise and partly by the government.

- Positive economic statements are facts which can be tested as true or false, whereas normative economic statements are value-judgements which cannot be tested as true or false.

What determines the demand for a good or service in a market?

Markets

A **market** is where buyers and sellers come into contact for the purpose of exchange. A price is agreed for exchange to take place. By price, we mean the exchange value of a good or service. There are many types of market and the Edexcel specification focuses on product, commodity and labour markets.

A product market refers to goods or services which the consumer derives utility from — they are wanted for their own sake. Examples are chocolate, wine and fast food.

A commodity market refers to raw materials or minerals used in the production of goods and services. Examples are wheat, sugar, oil and gold.

A labour market refers to the buying and selling of labour time for the production of goods and services. Examples include the markets for plumbers, teachers and accountants.

Demand

The buyers or consumers in a market are said to demand goods or services. **Demand** refers to the quantity of a good or service purchased at a given price over a given time period.

Demand is different from just wanting a good or service. It is a want backed up by the ability to pay, which is also known as effective demand.

Downward-sloping demand curve

A **demand curve** is the quantity of a good or service that would be bought over a range of different price levels in a given period of time.

The demand curve slopes downwards from left to right for two reasons:

(1) The substitution effect. When the price of a good falls, it becomes cheaper relative to its substitutes and some consumers switch their purchases from more expensive substitutes to the good in question.

(2) The income effect. When the price of a good falls, the real income of a consumer may rise. In effect, the purchasing power of the consumer's nominal income has increased and so more of the good can be bought.

Knowledge check 7

Why does the demand curve slope downwards from left to right?

The market demand curve is the horizontal summation of each individual demand curve for a particular good or service.

Movement along a demand curve

There is a movement along a demand curve for a good *only* when there is a change in its price. A fall in price causes an **extension** in demand, and a rise in price causes a **contraction** in demand, as shown in Figure 4.

Knowledge check 8

What causes a movement along a demand curve for a good?

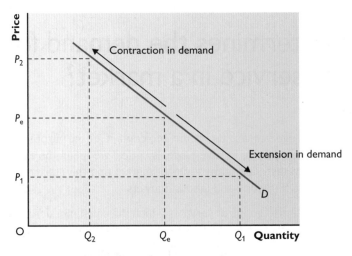

Figure 4 Movement along a demand curve

Shifts in the demand curve

An **increase** in demand refers to the whole demand curve shifting outwards to the right at every price level. A **decrease** in demand refers to the whole demand curve shifting inwards to the left at every price level.

There are various factors which can shift the demand curve for a good. For example, the demand for Sony PlayStation games consoles might increase due to:
- a fall in the price of complementary goods, such as computer games (Grand Theft Auto and FIFA Soccer)
- a rise in the price of substitute goods, such as the Microsoft Xbox 360 or the Nintendo Wii games consoles
- a change in fashion and tastes which make games consoles more popular as a leisure activity among young people
- increased advertising of PlayStation games and consoles
- an increase in real incomes (for normal goods) meaning that the PlayStation becomes more affordable for people to buy
- a decrease in income tax which leads to an increase in disposable income so that a PlayStation becomes more affordable
- an increase in the population or a change in the age structure of the population so that there are more teenagers likely to purchase a PlayStation
- an increase in credit facilities which makes it easier to obtain funds to pay for a PlayStation games console

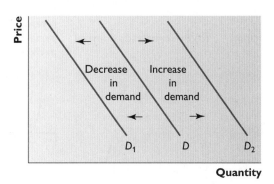

Figure 5 Shifts in demand curves

Figure 5 shows a decrease in demand by the shift of the demand curve leftwards to D_1 and an increase in demand is demonstrated by a rightward shift to D_2.

Price, income and cross elasticity of demand

Price elasticity of demand

Price elasticity of demand (PED) is the responsiveness in the demand for a good due to a change in its price. The formula to calculate it is:

$$\text{PED} = \frac{\text{percentage change in quantity demanded of good A}}{\text{percentage change in price of good A}}$$

Knowledge check 9

What causes a shift in the demand curve for a good?

Examiner tip

Make sure you can calculate percentages and percentage change from data, since there is usually a calculation question on the Unit I exam paper.

Knowledge check 10

What does the minus sign
mean in price elasticity of
demand answers?

In most circumstances, a minus answer is obtained, indicating that the two variables
of price and demand move in opposite directions. There is a negative gradient.

Types of price elasticity of demand

If PED is greater than 1, the good is price elastic: that is, the percentage change
in demand is greater than the percentage change in price. For example, a 10% rise in
the price of holidays to Florida may cause a 20% decrease in the quantity demanded;
PED is −2.

If PED is less than 1, the good is price inelastic: that is, the percentage change in
demand is less than the percentage change in price. For example, a 10% fall in price
of coffee may cause a 5% increase in the quantity demanded; PED is −0.5.

If PED is equal to 1, the good has unit elasticity: that is, the percentage change in
demand is the same as the percentage change in price. For example, a 10% fall in the
price of apples may cause a 10% rise in the quantity demanded; PED is −1.

If PED is equal to zero, the good is perfectly inelastic: that is, a change in price has
no effect on the quantity demanded. The demand curve is vertical. An example might
be heroin to a drug addict.

If PED is infinite, the good is perfectly elastic: that is, a rise in price causes demand
to fall to zero. The demand curve is horizontal.

The demand curves in Figure 6 show the different elasticities.

Knowledge check 11

What does the actual
figure represent in price
elasticity of demand
answers?

Examiner tip

Do not confuse elasticity
with the gradient of a
demand curve. Straight-
line demand curves have
constant gradients but
different elasticities along
them.

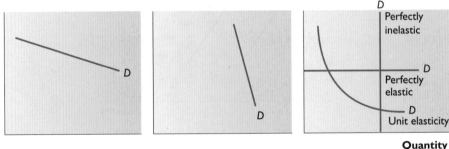

Figure 6 Different price elasticities of demand

The relationship between price elasticity of demand and total revenue

Elasticity varies along a straight-line demand curve, as shown in Figure 7. Elasticity
falls as you move along the curve from the top left to the bottom right. At the mid-
point, demand has unit elasticity.

Edexcel AS Economics

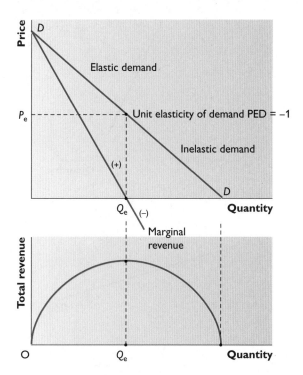

Figure 7 The relationship between price elasticity of demand and total revenue

Total revenue

Total revenue refers to the total payments a firm receives from selling a given quantity of goods or services. It is the price per unit of a good multiplied by the quantity sold. The total revenue a firm receives from selling a good will be equal to the total spending by consumers on that good.

A firm's **total revenue will increase** as long as **price is moving towards the mid-position of the demand curve** (where there is **unit elasticity**). It is important for firms to know the PED of their output when making pricing decisions, because this affects revenue and profitability.

If demand is elastic, then a cut in price increases total consumer spending and hence revenue to the firm. On the other hand, a rise in price causes total consumer spending to fall and so firms lose revenue.

If demand is inelastic, then an increase in price increases total consumer spending and hence revenue to the firm. On the other hand, a fall in price causes total consumer spending to fall and so firms lose revenue.

Once unit price elasticity has been reached, the firm is maximising its total revenue. Note the relationship between PED and marginal revenue, which falls during a move down the demand curve. As long as marginal revenue is positive, demand is price elastic. When marginal revenue is zero, demand is unit elastic; when marginal revenue is negative, demand is inelastic.

Knowledge check 12

Why might price elasticity of demand be useful to firms?

Knowledge check 13

Why might price elasticity of demand be useful to the government?

Examiner tip

Be prepared to draw a diagram to show how a change in price will affect total revenue. For example, a rise in price will increase total revenue from OP_eXQ_e to OP_2YQ_2 when demand is inelastic (Figure 8); a fall in price will increase total revenue from OP_eXQ_e to OP_1WQ_1 when demand is elastic (Figure 9).

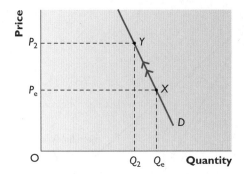

Figure 8 A rise in price increases total revenue under inelastic demand

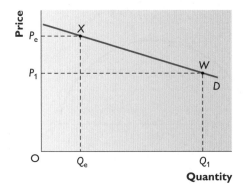

Figure 9 A fall in price increases total revenue under elastic demand

Determinants of price elasticity of demand

- **Availability of substitutes.** The more narrowly a good is defined, the more substitutes it tends to have and so its demand is elastic. For example, cod, a type of fish, has many substitutes such as plaice, rock, salmon and haddock. However, the more broadly a good is defined, the fewer substitutes it tends to have and so demand is less elastic. For example, there are few close substitutes for fish as a whole and so demand tends to be relatively less elastic.
- **Luxury and necessity goods.** Luxury goods, such as racing cars and caviar, tend to have an elastic demand, whereas necessity goods, like bread and underwear, tend to have an inelastic demand.
- **Proportion of income spent on the good.** If a high percentage of income is spent on the good, as with a new car or boat, demand tends to be price elastic. However, for goods that take up a small percentage of income, such as newspapers and tomato sauce, demand will tend to be price inelastic.
- **Addictive and habit-forming goods.** Tobacco, alcohol and coffee are the type of goods that tend to be price inelastic in demand.
- **The time period.** For most goods demand is less elastic in the short run than in the long run. For example, a rise in the price of household electricity is likely to have only a minor effect on consumption in the short run. In the long run, households can cut back on consumption by switching to gas for their cooking

and heating. This means demand eventually becomes more responsive to changes in price.

- **Brand image.** Some goods have a strong brand image, for example, Levi jeans and Coca Cola. Demand is typically price inelastic as consumers are often willing to pay a premium price for these products.

Income elasticity of demand

Income elasticity of demand (YED) is the responsiveness of demand for a good or service to a change in real income. (Real income refers to the spending power of money income — the amount of goods and services which can be purchased with one's nominal income.) The formula to calculate YED is:

$$YED = \frac{\text{percentage change in demand for a good}}{\text{percentage change in real income}}$$

Normal goods

In most circumstances YED is positive, which means the two variables of income and demand move in the same direction. In other words, a rise in income causes a rise in quantity demanded.

Inferior goods

Occasionally, YED is negative which means the two variables of income and demand move in opposite directions. This is because people tend to demand higher-quality goods as their incomes rise, substituting them for lower-quality products. Figure 10 shows the demand curve for an inferior good compared with that of a normal good in relation to income.

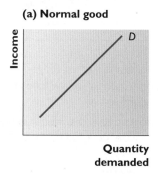
(a) Normal good

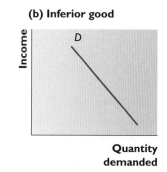
(b) Inferior good

Figure 10 Income elasticity of demand

Cross elasticity of demand

Cross elasticity of demand (XED) is the responsiveness of demand for good B to a change in price of good A. The formula to calculate XED is:

$$XED = \frac{\text{percentage change in demand for good B}}{\text{percentage change in price of good A}}$$

Cross elasticity of demand is used to determine whether goods are complements or substitutes for each other.

Substitute goods

Substitute goods are in competitive demand. For example, a rise in the price of coffee may cause an increase in demand for tea. XED is positive for substitute goods, as the two variables of price and demand move in the same direction. There is a positive gradient.

Complementary goods

Complementary goods are in joint demand. They tend to be consumed together. For example, a fall in the price of tennis rackets may cause an increase in demand for tennis balls. XED is negative for complementary goods, as the two variables of price and demand move in opposite directions. There is a negative gradient.

Figure 11 demonstrates cross elasticity of demand for complementary goods and substitute goods.

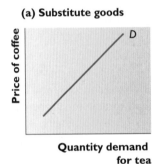

(a) Substitute goods

Price of coffee / Quantity demand for tea

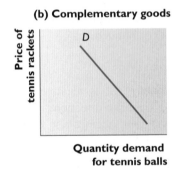

(b) Complementary goods

Price of tennis rackets / Quantity demand for tennis balls

Figure 11 Cross elasticity of demand

What determines the supply of a good or service in a market?

Supply

The sellers or producers in a market are said to supply goods and services. **Supply** refers to the quantity of a good or service that firms are willing to sell at a given price and over a given period of time.

An upward-sloping supply curve

A **supply curve** is the quantity of a good or service that firms are willing to sell to a market over a range of different price levels in a given period of time. The supply curve slopes upwards from left to right for two reasons:

(1) As price rises, it encourages firms to supply more of a good to make more profit.

(2) As firms raise output in the short run, they face rising production costs. To cover the rising costs, firms need to be able to charge higher prices to consumers. Higher prices can enable marginal firms to enter a market.

The market supply curve is the horizontal summation of individual firms' supply curves for a particular good or service.

Movement along a supply curve

There is movement along a supply curve for a good *only* when there is a change in its price. A rise in price causes an **extension** in supply, and a fall in price causes a **contraction** in supply, as shown in Figure 12.

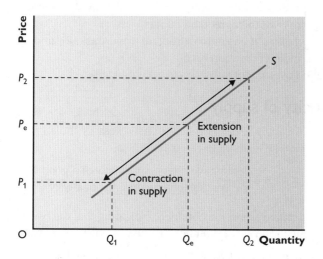

Figure 12 Movement along a supply curve

> **Knowledge check 16**
>
> Why does the supply curve slope upwards from left to right?

> **Knowledge check 17**
>
> What causes a movement along a supply curve for a good?

Shifts in the supply curve

An **increase** in supply refers to the whole supply curve shifting outwards to the right at every price level (to S_2 in Figure 13). A **decrease** in supply refers to the whole supply curve shifting inwards to the left at every level (to S_1 in Figure 13).

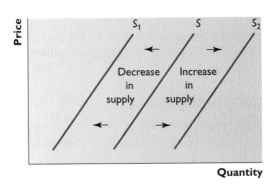

Figure 13 Shifts in the supply curve

There are various factors that can shift the supply curve of a good. For example, the supply of oil could increase due to:

- improvements in technology, e.g. the extraction of oil from more difficult places (under the sea bed in deeper water)
- a reduction in labour costs, e.g. lower wages for oil platform and oil refinery workers
- a reduction in capital costs, e.g. oil platforms, pipelines and refineries
- a reduction in transport costs, e.g. an increase in size of oil tankers
- discovery of new oil fields, e.g. in the Falklands and Uganda
- an increase in the number of firms in the oil industry
- a decrease in the market influences of OPEC (Organisation of Petroleum Exporting Countries), a producer cartel. (This may occur if individual member states decide to produce more than the agreed oil quotas.)
- good weather making it easier to extract oil from Alaska or under the sea bed
- a reduction in indirect taxation on oil
- an increase in government subsidies to oil producers

Knowledge check 18

What causes a shift in the supply curve for a good?

Price elasticity of supply

Price elasticity of supply (PES) is the responsiveness of the supply of a good to a change in its price. The formula to calculate PES is:

$$PES = \frac{\text{percentage change in supply of a good}}{\text{percentage change in price of a good}}$$

In most cases a positive answer is obtained, indicating that the two variables of price and quantity move in the same direction. There is a positive gradient.

If PES is greater than 1, the good is price elastic: that is, the percentage change in supply is greater than the percentage change in price of the good.

If PES is less than 1, the good is price inelastic: that is, the percentage change in supply is less than the percentage change in price of the good.

Knowledge check 19

What does a positive figure mean in price elasticity of supply answers?

If PES is equal to 1, the good is unit elastic: that is, the percentage change in supply is the same as the percentage change in price of the good.

If PES is equal to zero, the good is perfectly inelastic: that is, a change in price has no effect on the quantity supplied. The supply curve is vertical.

If PES is infinite, the good is perfectly elastic. The supply curve is horizontal.

Figure 14 shows the different price elasticities of supply.

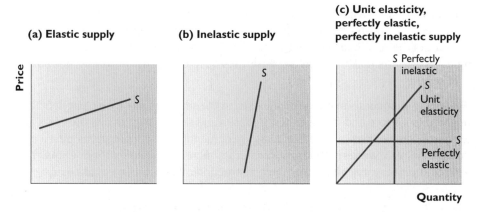

Figure 14 Different price elasticities of supply

Knowledge check 20

What does the 'number' represent in price elasticity of supply answers?

Determinants of price elasticity of supply

- **Level of spare capacity.** A high level of spare capacity in a firm means that it can raise production quickly, so supply tends to be elastic. A firm or industry operating at full capacity is unable to raise output quickly and so supply tends to be inelastic.
- **The state of the economy.** In a recession there are many unemployed resources and so there is a high level of spare capacity. Firms find it relatively easy to raise supply if needed.
- **Level of stocks of finished goods in a firm.** A high level of stocks means that the firm can increase supply quickly, so supply is elastic: for example, US motor vehicle manufacturers often have stockpiles of cars waiting to sell. Alternatively, a firm or industry operating with low stocks is unable to raise output quickly and so supply tends to be inelastic. This is more likely to be the case for a firm making designer wedding dresses.
- **Perishability of the product.** Some goods cannot be stockpiled: for example, some agricultural goods such as fresh fruit, vegetables and flowers are highly perishable. These goods are typically inelastic in supply. On the other hand, manufactured goods tend to be non-perishable and so can be stockpiled by firms in order to meet anticipated increases in demand. Examples are household electrical goods such as fridges, freezers and washing machines.
- **The ease of entry to an industry.** If there are high entry barriers to an industry then it will be difficult for new firms to enter, even with the attraction of high prices and profits. Sometimes existing producers deliberately create entry barriers, so supply may be restricted and inelastic.

Examiner tip

Be careful not to confuse the determinants of price elasticity of supply with those of price elasticity of demand. This is one of the most common mistakes examiners encounter when marking elasticity of supply questions.

Knowledge check 21

How might the price elasticity of supply for a good change over time?

Examiner tip

Be prepared to draw a diagram to show how price elasticity of supply may vary over time, to support your answer (see Figure 15). Usually 1 mark is available for this.

- **The time period under consideration.** This is perhaps the most important determinant of elasticity of supply. The short run is the period of time in which a firm is able to increase supply with its existing capacity. At least one factor input is likely to be fixed in quantity in the short run, which makes it difficult for a firm to raise production. Supply tends to be relatively inelastic. The long run is the period of time in which a firm is able to increase supply by adding to its production capacity. All factor inputs are variable in the long run, making it easier for a firm to raise production. Supply tends to be relatively elastic.

For many agricultural products, supply is inelastic in the short run because the output from the summer and autumn harvests depends on the amount of seed planted at the start of the year. It takes an even longer period of time to raise the supply of dairy products such as milk and beef because these depend on the nurturing of animals over several years.

The supply of minerals may also be inelastic in the short run due to the length of time required to explore and discover new deposits and then extract them. The costs and technical complexities involved could be phenomenal: for example, developing a new iron ore mine in Western Australia to cater for increasing demand from China. This will require heavy machinery and the construction of new rail and road links.

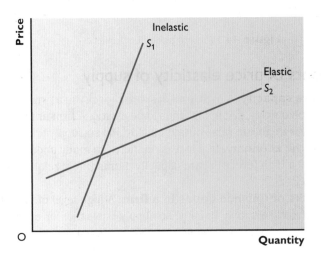

Figure 15 Elasticity of supply

Summary

- A movement along a supply curve is caused by a change in the price of the good, whereas shifts in a supply curve are caused by other factors: for example, changes in costs of production, technology, the ability of firms to enter and exit an industry, indirect taxes and government subsidies.
- The determinants of price elasticity of supply of a good include the level of spare capacity, the state of

the economy, level of stocks, perishability, ease of entry and exit to an industry and the time period under consideration.
- A vertical supply curve indicates that supply of a good is perfectly inelastic: for example, the capacity of Wembley stadium is 90,000 seats.

What determines the equilibrium price or wage in a market?

Equilibrium in a market

Equilibrium means there is a balance in the market, with no tendency for price or output to change. The equilibrium price and quantity of a good are obtained from the point of intersection between the demand and supply curves. In the table below and Figure 16, the equilibrium price is £80 per unit and the quantity is 30 units per week.

Price	Quantity demanded per week	Quantity supplied per week
£100	10	50
£90	20	40
£80	30	30
£70	40	20
£60	50	10

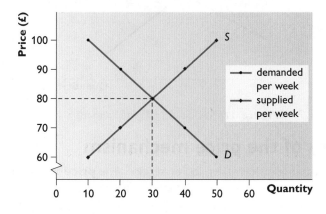

Figure 16 Market equilibrium

Excess supply and excess demand

In a free market, price cannot remain above or below the equilibrium position for long. For example, at a price of £100 there is an **excess supply** of 40 units. In order to sell the surplus, producers tend to reduce price and this encourages consumers to buy more. Demand extends and supply contracts until the equilibrium price of £80 is reached.

At a price of £60 there is an **excess demand** of 40 units. Consumers tend to bid up the price in order to obtain the good and this encourages producers to supply more. Supply extends and demand contracts until the equilibrium price of £80 is reached. Thus, the price mechanism automatically eliminates surpluses and shortages of a good, something that the economist Adam Smith referred to as the 'invisible hand' of the market.

Knowledge check 22

What is likely to happen to the price of a good if supply exceeds demand in a free market?

Knowledge check 23

What is likely to happen to the price of a good if demand exceeds supply in a free market?

Knowledge check 24

Briefly explain how an increase in supply of a good affects consumer surplus.

Knowledge check 25

Briefly explain how a decrease in demand for a good affects producer surplus.

Examiner tip

For multiple-choice questions on consumer surplus or producer surplus, where a diagram is provided, you should always state the original area, the new area and the actual increase or decrease in area. This could be done by annotating the diagram.

Examiner tip

The most effective way to explain the functions of the price mechanism is by using a demand and supply diagram. For example, an increase in demand for gold will raise its price and offer a profit incentive for more to be supplied to the market. The rise in price also acts as a signal to the market for more to be produced.

Consumer and producer surplus

Consumer surplus is the extra amount of money consumers are prepared to pay for a good or service above what they actually pay. It is the utility or satisfaction gained from a good or service in excess of that paid for it.

Producer surplus is the extra amount of money paid to producers above what they are willing to accept to supply a good or service. It is the extra earnings obtained by a producer above the minimum required to supply the good or service.

The areas of consumer and producer surplus are shown in Figure 17. Consumer surplus is the area above the equilibrium price but below the demand curve; producer surplus is the area below the equilibrium price and above the supply curve.

Note that a shift in the demand or supply curve, leading to a new market price, will cause the amount of both consumer and producer surplus to change.

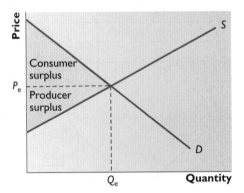

Figure 17 Consumer and producer surplus

Functions of the price mechanism

Price is the exchange value of a good or service. The **price mechanism** refers to the way price responds to changes in demand or supply for a product or factor input, so that a new equilibrium position is reached in a market. It is the principal method of allocating resources in a market economy. The price mechanism has several functions:

- **A rationing device.** Resources are scarce, which means that the goods and services produced from them are limited in supply. The price mechanism allocates these goods and services to those who are prepared to pay the most for them. In effect, price will rise or fall until equilibrium is reached between the quantity demanded and quantity supplied.
- **An incentive device.** Rising prices tend to act as an incentive to firms to produce more of a good or service, since higher profits can be earned. Rising prices also mean firms are able to cover the extra costs involved with increasing output.
- **A signalling device.** The price mechanism indicates changes in the conditions of demand or supply. For example, an increase in demand for a good or service raises its price and encourages firms to expand their supply, while a decrease in demand lowers the price and causes firms to contract their supply. Consequently, more or fewer resources are allocated to the production of a particular good or service.

Any of the factors which may shift demand or supply curves will lead to a change in price of a good or service. The role of indirect taxes and subsidies in influencing price is now considered in more detail.

Indirect taxes

A tax is a compulsory charge made by the government, on goods, services, incomes or capital. The purpose is to raise funds to pay for government spending programmes. There are two types of tax: direct and indirect.

A **direct tax** is levied directly on an individual or organisation. Direct taxes are generally paid on incomes: for example, personal income tax and corporation tax (on company profits).

An **indirect tax** is usually levied on the purchase of goods and services. It represents a tax on expenditure. There are two types of indirect tax: specific and *ad valorem* taxes. A specific tax is charged as a fixed amount per unit of a good, such as a litre of wine or a packet of cigarettes. An excise tax is a good example. An *ad valorem* tax is charged as a percentage of the price of a good: for example, VAT of 20% is added on to restaurant meals.

The imposition of an indirect tax raises the price of a good or service. The tax is added to the supply price, effectively causing the supply curve to shift vertically upwards and to the left (a decrease in supply). A **specific tax** causes a parallel shift of the supply curve to the left, as shown in part (a) of Figure 18. An ***ad valorem* tax** causes a pivotal rotation of the supply curve to the left, as shown in part (b).

Knowledge check 26

Distinguish between a specific tax and an *ad valorem* tax.

(a) Specific tax

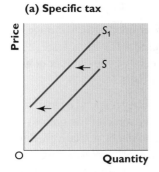

(b) *Ad valorem* tax

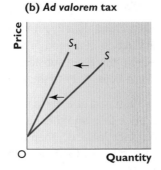

Figure 18 Specific tax and *ad valorem* tax

The incidence of an indirect tax

The tax incidence usually falls partly on consumers and partly on producers, depending on the relative price elasticities of demand and supply for the good or service. A combination of price inelastic demand and price elastic supply tends to place most of the tax burden on consumers; addictive goods such as tobacco and alcohol tend to be price inelastic in demand. This means that firms are able to pass most of the burden of tax on to consumers via higher prices.

However, a combination of price elastic demand and price inelastic supply tends to place most of the tax burden on the producers. It may also lead to a significant

Content guidance

reduction in output and employment. Consequently, a government may be reluctant to place high indirect taxes on these types of goods or services.

Figure 19 shows the effects of a specific tax on a good. Before the tax, equilibrium price is P_e and quantity Q_e. After the tax is imposed, the supply curve shifts to S_1 and the equilibrium price rises to P_1 while quantity falls to Q_1. The total tax area is $XYWP_1$.

The incidence of tax paid by consumers is shown by the actual rise in market price from P_e to P_1. Consumers pay the amount of tax shown by the area XZP_eP_1. The tax paid by producers is the remaining area $ZYWP_e$.

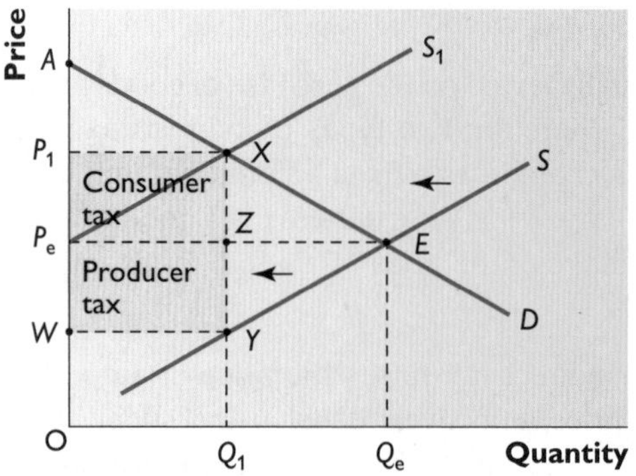

Figure 19 The incidence of taxation

Subsidies

A **subsidy** is a grant, usually provided by the government, to encourage suppliers to increase production of a good or service, leading to a fall in its price. Bus and train companies are often given subsidies in order to increase the number of bus and train services, which benefits both the firms and consumers.

A subsidy is often paid directly to producers, but as they respond by increasing output, the market price falls and this indirectly passes on some of the gain to consumers. If demand is price inelastic, then the market price falls by a relatively large amount, increasing the benefits to consumers. If demand is price elastic, then market price falls by a relatively small amount and so there is less gain for consumers. Figure 20 shows the imposition of a government subsidy for a good.

Before the subsidy, equilibrium price is P_e and quantity Q_e. After the subsidy is imposed, the supply curve shifts to S_2 and equilibrium price falls to P_2 while the quantity rises to Q_2. The total subsidy area is $RLGP_2$.

The amount of subsidy that consumers gain is shown by the actual fall in market price from P_e to P_2. They gain by paying a lower price for the good. The consumer subsidy area is RTP_eP_2. The remaining subsidy area of $TLGP_e$ represents the gain made by producers.

Examiner tip
One way of working out the proportion of an indirect tax paid by consumers is to consider the actual increase in market price of a good once the tax is imposed. After all, consumers pay the market price. The rest of the tax is then paid by producers.

Examiner tip
One way of working out the proportion of a subsidy that is gained by consumers is to consider the actual fall in market price once the subsidy is applied. The reduction in price is the part of the subsidy from which consumers directly benefit. The rest of the subsidy remains with producers.

Knowledge check 27
How does a unit subsidy affect the market for a good?

26

Edexcel AS Economics

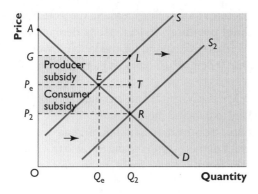

Figure 20 A government subsidy to producers

Wage determination

In a competitive labour market the wage rate is determined by the interaction of demand and supply. The demand for labour is undertaken by firms, which require workers to help produce goods and services. The supply of labour comes from the general population and, in particular, the workforce of an economy.

In practice there are many different types of labour market: for example, shop assistants, kitchen chefs and lawyers. Labour markets also include public sector workers where the government is a major employer of labour: for example, teachers, nurses and police officers.

The demand for labour

The demand for labour is a **derived demand**. It is derived from the demand for the goods and services it makes. For example, the demand for building workers is derived from the demand for new housing.

Figure 21 shows how an increase in demand for new housing will cause an increase in demand for building workers, such as bricklayers and carpenters. The effect is to increase the wage rate from W_e to W_1 and the quantity employed from N_e to N_1.

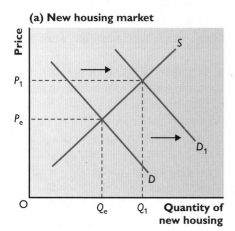
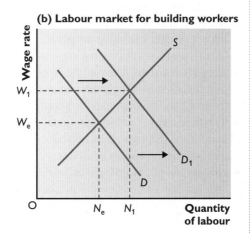

Figure 21 An increase in the demand for new housing and building workers

There are several key determinants of the demand for labour:

- **Demand for the final product.** An increase in demand for a good or service is likely to cause an increase in demand for the labour involved in making it. Firms have a profit incentive, if demand and prices increase, to supply more of a good or service.
- **The wage rate.** A fall in the wage rate means that labour becomes more affordable and so firms are likely to demand more labour.
- **Other labour costs.** For example, a fall in employers' national insurance contributions on behalf of their staff is likely to raise the quantity demanded.
- **Price of other factor inputs.** An increase in the price of capital might encourage firms to employ more labour and cut back on the use of machinery and equipment where possible. This is because labour and capital may be substitutes in the production process.
- **Productivity of labour.** An increase in output per worker may lead to higher revenue and profits, encouraging firms to employ more people.
- **Government employment regulations.** The fewer the number of regulations, the greater the demand for labour is likely to be. For example, if it becomes easy to hire and fire staff or to change working conditions, then the increased labour flexibility may encourage firms to employ more people. However, a national minimum wage (NMW) set above the free-market wage may cause a decrease in the quantity of labour demanded.

Knowledge check 28

What is meant by derived demand?

The supply of labour

This refers to the quantity and quality of labour hours offered for work over a given time period. There are various factors which determine the supply of labour, namely:

- **The wage rate.** An increase in the wage rate will encourage more people to offer their services for work. A higher wage rate means the opportunity cost of leisure time increases, encouraging people to work longer hours.
- **Other net advantages of work.** Improvements in working conditions will also tend to increase the supply of labour: for example, a good pension, paid holidays, job security and promotion prospects.
- **Net migration.** Over recent years the UK has experienced a significant increase in immigration from central and eastern Europe, helping to boost the economy.
- **Income tax.** A reduction in income tax will increase disposable incomes and so offer a greater incentive for people to work. Many people will substitute work for leisure time, increasing the supply of labour.
- **Benefit reform.** A reduction in benefits (e.g. incapacity benefit, housing benefit and the jobseeker's allowance) may provide a greater incentive for people to look for work and so increase the supply of labour.
- **Trade unions.** Trade unions act to increase wage rates and improve other working conditions through collective bargaining with employers. This may encourage an increase in the supply of labour.
- **Government regulations.** An increase in employment protection or the introduction of a national minimum wage will tend to improve working conditions and so increase the supply of labour. However, it is also possible that government regulations reduce the supply of labour (for example, the EU Work Time Directive limits the maximum hours of work per week to 48 for most employees).

Examiner tip

One evaluation technique is to prioritise among different factors: for example, discussing the factors which determine the supply of labour to a particular occupation. The supply of labour to accountancy is more likely to be influenced by the availability of training courses and the skills required than by the role of trade unions.

- **Social trends.** There has been a significant increase in the number of women in the workforce over the past 40 years. This reflects an improvement in equal opportunities, childcare facilities and social attitudes.

The National Minimum Wage (NMW)

- The NMW refers to the legal minimum hourly rate of pay an employer can pay its workers. In effect, it is a floor wage which protects workers in low-paid occupations such as shop assistants, cleaners and laundries. If the NMW is set above the free-market equilibrium in a particular labour market then it may cause unemployment. Figure 22 shows how the NMW causes a contraction in demand from ON_e to ON_1 and an extension in supply from ON_e to ON_2, leading to an excess supply of labour N_1N_2.

Knowledge check 29

What is the impact of an NMW set below the market equilibrium wage in a labour market?

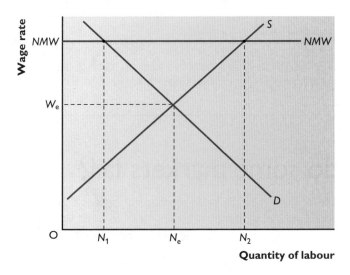

Figure 22 National Minimum Wage

Advantages of increasing the NMW

- A reduction in exploitation of labour and poverty.
- A reduction in wage inequality between men and women. Women tend to be disproportionately represented in low-paid occupations and so benefit most from an increase in NMW.
- A reduction in voluntary unemployment since there is more incentive to take low-paid work.
- An increase in labour productivity as workers become more satisfied in their jobs. Firms may also increase training of workers in order to increase productivity and so justify paying the higher wage.
- To keep up with an increase in the cost of living due to inflation.

Disadvantages of increasing the NMW

- Increases in unemployment since firms find it too expensive to employ labour. Workers may be replaced with capital in the production process, for example, self-service tills in supermarkets.

Examiner tip

One way to evaluate the effects of an increase in the NMW is to use the concept of elasticity. A wage-inelastic demand for labour will lead to relatively few job losses. It means workers are hard to replace in production, as in the case of cleaners. A wage-elastic demand for labour will lead to relatively more job losses. It means workers are easier to replace in production, as with supermarket cashiers.

- An increase in inflationary pressure as firms pass on the extra wage costs to consumers in the form of higher prices for their products.
- An ineffective means of reducing poverty since many poor people do not work, for example, the unemployed, sick and elderly. Similarly, many people who benefit from the NMW may not be from poor households (such as students and second wage earners).
- An increase in red tape or bureaucracy for firms leading to higher costs and less flexibility in the labour market. This may represent government failure.

Summary

- In a competitive market the price of a good or service is determined by the interaction of demand and supply.
- An excess demand for a good will cause price to rise until equilibrium is reached; an excess supply of a good will cause price to fall until equilibrium is reached.
- An indirect tax on a good will cause an inward shift in the supply curve, leading to a fall in output and a rise in price.
- A unit subsidy on a good will cause an outward shift in the supply curve, leading to a rise in output and a fall in price.
- In a competitive labour market the wage rate is determined by the interaction of demand and supply.
- The National Minimum Wage may help to reduce poverty and exploitation of labour but could also lead to unemployment.

Why do some markets fail?

Market failure occurs when the price mechanism causes an inefficient allocation of resources; the forces of demand and supply lead to a net welfare loss in society. Consequently, resources are not allocated to their best or optimum use.

There are various types of market failure and you may come across different classifications in your textbooks. However, the Edexcel Unit 1 specification focuses on the following: externalities, public goods, imperfect market information, labour immobility and unstable commodity markets.

Externalities

Externalities are those costs or benefits which are external to an exchange. They are third party effects ignored by the price mechanism.

Externalities are also known as *indirect costs* and *benefits*, or as *spillovers from production* or *consumption* of a good or service. In effect, external costs are *negative externalities* and external benefits are *positive externalities*.

External costs

External costs may occur in the production and the consumption of a good or service. An example of an external cost in production is a chemical firm polluting a river with its waste. This causes an external cost to the fishing and water supply industries. Fish catches may be reduced and it may become very expensive to purify water to meet the European Commission's safety standards.

Examiner tip

When defining external costs, offer two ideas as there are often 2 marks available: for example, 'They are negative third party effects and represent costs outside of the market transaction.' Also be prepared to give an example, such as air pollution from the production of cement.

An example of an external cost in consumption is a person smoking tobacco, polluting the air for others. The effect is to cause passive smoking, where non-smokers may suffer the same illnesses as smokers.

Private costs

In a free market, producers are only concerned with the private costs of production. These are costs internal to the firm, which it directly pays for. These costs include wages for workers, rent of buildings, payment for raw materials, machinery costs, electricity and gas costs, insurance, packaging and transport costs from running lorries. Private costs may also refer to the market price that a consumer pays for a good or service.

Social costs

By adding private costs to external costs we obtain social costs. This means that external costs are the difference between private costs and social costs. The marginal private cost and marginal social cost curves often diverge, indicating that external costs increase disproportionately with output. However, it is possible that external costs per unit of output remain constant, in which case the marginal private cost and marginal social cost curves are drawn parallel to each other. The relationship between private cost, external cost and social cost is shown in Figure 23.

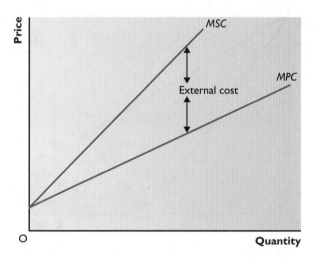

Figure 23 The relationship between private cost, external cost and social cost in the production of a good

Knowledge check 30

What are social costs?

Note that the Edexcel specification focuses on diagrammatic analysis of external costs in production.

External benefits

External benefits may occur in the production and consumption of a good or service. An example of an external benefit in production is the recycling of waste materials such as newspapers, glass and tins. It has the benefit of reducing the amount of waste disposal for landfill sites as well as re-using materials for production. It helps to promote sustainable economic growth.

An external benefit in consumption is the vaccination of an individual against various diseases. It reduces the possibility of other people catching a disease who come into contact with the vaccinated individual.

Private benefits

In a free market, consumers are only concerned with the private benefits or utility from consuming a good or service. Economists assume this can be measured by the price that consumers are prepared to pay for a good or service. Private benefits may also refer to the revenue that a firm obtains from selling a good or service.

Social benefits

By adding private benefits to external benefits we obtain social benefits. This means external benefits are the difference between private benefits and social benefits. The marginal private benefit and marginal social benefit curves often diverge, indicating that external benefits increase disproportionately with output consumed, as shown in Figure 24. However, it is possible that external benefit per unit consumed will remain constant, in which case the marginal private benefit and marginal social benefit curves are drawn parallel to each other.

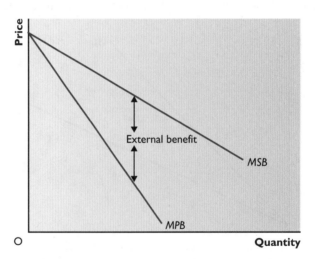

Figure 24 The private benefits, external benefits and social benefits from the consumption of a good

Note that the Edexcel specification focuses on diagrammatic analysis of external benefits in consumption of goods and services.

The free-market equilibrium

The supply curve for a firm is the marginal private cost curve (*MPC*). The addition of all the *MPC* curves of firms in a market for a particular good or service will form the market supply curve.

The demand curve for consumers is the marginal private benefit curve (*MPB*). Economists assume that it is possible to measure the benefit obtained from consuming a good by the price people are prepared to pay for it. As an individual consumes more units of a good, the marginal benefit (marginal utility) will fall. This is why the demand curve slopes downwards from left to right. The addition of all the consumers' *MPB* curves for a particular good or service will form the market demand curve.

Market equilibrium occurs where marginal private benefit equals marginal private cost.

The social optimum equilibrium

The social optimum equilibrium level of output or price for a good or service occurs where marginal social cost (*MSC*) equals marginal social benefit (*MSB*). The social cost of producing the last unit of output equals the social benefit from consuming it. When the social optimum is reached in a market, welfare is maximised.

External costs and the triangle of welfare loss

The free market ignores negative externalities. However, adding external costs on to the production of a good or service, such as the production of chemical goods, causes the supply curve of the firm to shift to the left and become the marginal social cost curve, shown in Figure 25.

Assuming there are no external benefits in the production of a chemical good, the social optimum price is at OP_1 and quantity OQ_1. When external costs are ignored there is under-pricing and over-production. There is an excess of social costs over social benefits for the marginal output between Q_e and Q_1.

The marginal social cost of the output slice Q_eQ_1 is Q_eWYQ_1, which exceeds the marginal social benefit of this output Q_eXYQ_1. The excess of social costs over social benefits is shown by the triangle XWY. This is the area of welfare loss to society; the market has failed since negative externalities are ignored.

Knowledge check 32

Distinguish between the market equilibrium and social optimum positions in a market.

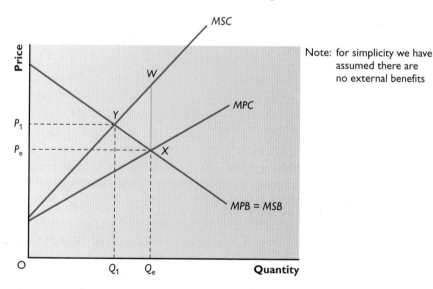

Note: for simplicity we have assumed there are no external benefits

Figure 25 External costs and the triangle of welfare loss

Knowledge check 33

What is the triangle of welfare loss?

External benefits and the triangle of welfare gain

The free market ignores positive externalities. However, adding external benefits on to the consumption of a good or service, such as the consumption of vaccinations, causes the demand curve to shift to the right and become the marginal social benefit curve, shown in Figure 26.

Assuming there are no external costs in the consumption of vaccinations in a free market, the social optimum price is at OP_2 and quantity OQ_2. When external benefits are ignored there is under-pricing and under-production. There is an excess of social benefits over social costs for the marginal output between Q_e and Q_2. Thus, by raising output from OQ_e to OQ_2, welfare could be increased.

The marginal social benefit of the output slice Q_eQ_2 is Q_eMTQ_2, which exceeds the marginal social cost of this output Q_eZTQ_2. The excess of social benefits over social costs is shown by the triangle MTZ. This is the area of welfare gain to society; the market has failed since positive externalities are ignored.

Knowledge check 34

What is the triangle of welfare gain?

Examiner tip

When inserting the area of welfare loss or welfare gain on an externality diagram, always start from the free-market equilibrium position and draw a line vertically up to the MSC or MSB curve. This will help delineate the area to shade in.

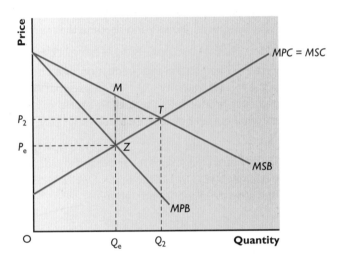

Figure 26 External benefits and the triangle of welfare gain

Public goods

Some goods may not be produced at all through the markets, despite offering significant benefits to society. Where this occurs it is known as a 'missing market' and the goods are called **public goods**. These goods involve a large element of collective consumption: for example, national defence, flood defence systems, the criminal justice system and refuse collection.

Public goods demonstrate characteristics of non-excludability and non-rivalry.
- **Non-excludability** means that once a good has been produced for the benefit of one person, it is impossible to stop others from benefiting.
- **Non-rivalry** means that as more people consume a good and enjoy its benefits, it does not reduce the amount available for others. In effect, it is non-diminishable.

Knowledge check 35

How are public goods defined?

Once a public good has been provided, the cost of supplying it to an extra consumer is zero. Further examples are firework displays, lighthouses, public beaches, public parks and street lighting.

Private goods

Private goods are the opposite of public goods. They display characteristics of rivalry and excludability in consumption. An example of a private good is a Mars bar, the consumption of which directly excludes other people from consuming that particular bar. The owners of private goods are able to use private property rights which prevent other people from consuming them. Private goods can also be rejected, which means one has a choice over whether to consume them or not.

The under-provision of public goods

Public goods are under-provided due to two problems.

(1) The free rider problem. Once a public good has been provided for one individual, it is automatically provided for all. The market fails because it is not possible for firms to withhold the good from those consumers who refuse to pay for it. Examples are national defence and security along a street.

The rational consumer would wait for someone else to provide the good and then reap the rewards by consuming it for free. However, if everyone waits for others to supply a public good then it may never be provided. The non-excludability characteristic means that the price mechanism cannot develop as free riders will not pay.

(2) The valuation problem. It is difficult to measure the value obtained by consumers of public goods and hence it becomes hard to establish a market price for them. It is in the interests of consumers to under-value the benefit gained from a public good so that they pay less for it; but it is in the interests of producers to over-value the benefit gained from a public good in order to charge more for it. The uncertainty over valuation may deter firms from providing public goods.

Government provision of public goods

In a mixed economy the government tends to provide public goods in order to correct market failure. It raises funds from general taxation to pay for their provision. Without government intervention, public goods may be under-provided or not provided at all. The actual quantity provided will be less than the amount required for achieving the social optimum position.

Imperfect market knowledge

Symmetric information

In the study of competitive markets it is often assumed that consumers and producers have perfect market information upon which to make their economic decisions. This is known as **symmetric information** — where consumers and producers have perfect and equal market information on a good or service. Assuming that consumers and producers act in a rational way, it will lead to an efficient allocation of resources.

Examiner tip

Do not make the mistake of calling the National Health Service and state education examples of public goods. There is rivalry in the consumption of these goods. It is more appropriate to describe them as goods which yield external benefits or merit goods.

Knowledge check 36

Why do public goods represent a type of market failure?

Asymmetric information

In reality, consumers and producers have imperfect and unequal market knowledge upon which to make their economic decisions and this could lead to a misallocation of resources. This is known as **asymmetric information**.

Often producers may know more than consumers about a good or service. A second-hand car salesman, for example, may have greater knowledge of the history of vehicles for sale as well as more technical knowledge than consumers. This could lead to a consumer paying too much for a poor-quality car. The fear of buying a defective car tends to reduce the market price for all second-hand cars, even the non-defective ones. Consequently the losers could be both buyers and sellers, depending on the car sold. This is known as a lemon market.

Sometimes consumers may have more market information than producers. For example, a consumer may purchase an insurance policy concealing information about himself or simply know more about his intended future actions. This might include a risky lifestyle.

When there is imperfect market information, markets are likely to fail. This can be seen in the under-consumption of healthcare, education and pensions (sometimes known as **merit goods**) or the over-consumption of tobacco, alcohol and gambling (sometimes known as **demerit goods**).

Knowledge check 37

Why does imperfect market knowledge lead to market failure?

Labour immobility

The **mobility of labour** refers to the ability of workers to change from one job to another, both geographically and occupationally. There are more than 30 million people working in UK labour markets producing a wide range of goods and services. However, over 2.5 million people are also unemployed, indicating that labour markets do not always operate efficiently.

Some of the unemployed may simply be changing jobs and so register as out of work for a short period of time. After all, the economy is dynamic and specialised, so we should expect some unemployment since jobs are continuously being created and ended. Unemployment while people search for jobs and fill them is known as **frictional unemployment**.

Knowledge check 38

Why does the immobility of labour lead to market failure?

However, a more serious type of unemployment is due to a mismatch of skills and location between job seekers and job providers. This gives rise to immobility of labour and **structural unemployment**.

Geographical immobility refers to the obstacles which prevent labour moving from one area to another to find work. There are several causes, such as family and social ties, the financial costs involved with moving home, imperfect market knowledge on available work, regional variations in house prices and the cost of living. The biggest problem tends to be the lack of affordable housing in many parts of the UK, but especially the southeast region.

Examiner tip

Do not confuse the 'mobility' of labour with 'immobility' of labour, otherwise your answer may be irrelevant to the question set.

Occupational immobility refers to the obstacles which prevent labour from changing their type of occupation to find work. There are several causes, including insufficient education, training, skills and work experience.

Government measures to increase labour mobility

There are various measures that a government might undertake to increase the geographical mobility of labour and these include:

- Relaxation of planning laws which enable construction firms to build housing, especially in green belt areas and the southeast of England.
- Increasing the construction of social housing, such as council properties and charities (housing associations). Rental costs tend to be more affordable than mortgages.
- Offering housing subsidies to certain groups of workers where acute shortages exist, such as teachers, nurses and fire fighters in southeast England. Subsidies may include mortgage relief, shared ownership and relocation grants.
- Improving the operation of Job Centres so that more information is available on job vacancies in any area.

The measures a government might use to increase the occupational mobility of labour include:

- Increasing the provision of training schemes, especially for the unemployed. This might include subsidies to private sector companies to offer training services.
- Increasing the provision of further education, especially in the post-16 sector. Vocational education courses offer training in specific work-based skills and work experience to students.
- Increasing the provision of higher education. There has been a rapid expansion in the number of students in this sector of education over recent years. Increasing access to student loans and limiting tuition fees might help here.

Unstable commodity markets

Commodities refer to raw materials used in the production of goods. They may be minerals and metals such as oil, coal, tin and copper or agricultural goods such as wheat, coffee, tea and sugar. Typically, commodities are used to manufacture goods and services.

Commodity markets are characterised by fluctuating prices and producer incomes which make it difficult to plan future investment programmes and production. This is best shown in agricultural markets where the climate may affect supply in any one year. In Figure 27, initially, planned output is Q_e and price P_e, leading to planned total revenue of OP_eXQ_e.

However, ideal weather increases supply to S_1, causing price to fall to P_1. (Supply is drawn as perfectly price inelastic since the length of the growing season means no more can be produced until the following year.) Total revenue also falls to OP_1YQ_1 since demand for agricultural commodities tends to be price inelastic. Indeed, agricultural goods are often used as ingredients for the production of food — a necessity. A 'good' harvest is a paradox, since farmers are likely to experience a fall in revenue and profits.

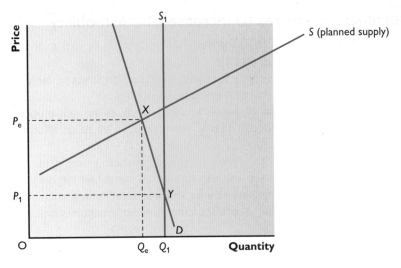

Figure 27 A good harvest (increase in supply)

Figure 28 shows a poor harvest due to bad weather, which decreases supply to S_2, causing price to rise to P_2. Total revenue also increases to OP_2WQ_2 since demand for agricultural commodities tends to be price inelastic. The 'poor' harvest is a paradox, since farmers are likely to experience a rise in revenue and profits.

Knowledge check 39

Why might a good harvest reduce total revenue and a poor harvest increase total revenue for farmers?

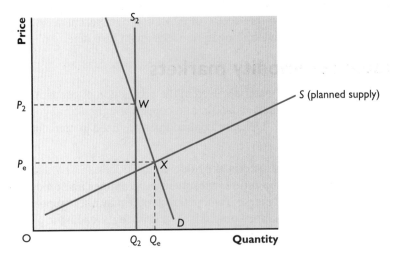

Figure 28 A poor harvest (decrease in supply)

The significance of price and income elasticity of demand

The problem of uncertain supply of commodities in any one year is compounded by the tendency for demand for this type of goods to be price inelastic. As shown previously, a good harvest will lead to a larger fall in price and revenue whereas a poor harvest will lead to a larger rise in price and total revenue. Consequently, farmers may make huge profits one year and huge losses another. It gives rise to market failure.

Examiner tip

There are many data-response questions on commodities. Be prepared to draw a diagram showing a rise in their price — a common cause is growing real incomes among the rapidly industrialising economies, which have led to increased demand.

In the long run, the supply of agricultural commodities has increased dramatically due to major technological innovations: for example, genetically modified crops which increase yield and resistance to drought and pests. However, the growth in demand has failed to keep up with supply. Commodities tend to be income inelastic in demand since each individual has a limited food intake. The implications point to further decreases in the real price of commodities and decreases in revenue for farmers.

However, the rapid economic growth of China and India has helped to increase the demand for commodities and so push up prices and revenues over recent years. The growth in use of bio fuels has also led to higher food prices.

The significance of time lags

The length of the growing season for agricultural commodities means there are **time lags** between farmers making the decision to sow seeds or raise livestock and the actual harvest of crops or sale of meat. In a free market this may cause cyclical fluctuations in prices and farm incomes.

> **Examiner tip**
> Agricultural commodities are typically price inelastic in supply in the short run due to the time taken to grow them. However, if spare stocks exist then supply could be price elastic in the short run as these can be released on to the market when price rises.

Summary

- There are various forms of market failure: for example, externalities, public goods, imperfect market information, labour immobility and unstable commodity markets.
- External costs and benefits arise due to third party effects in market transactions that the price mechanism ignores.
- Public goods would not be provided in a free-market economy due to the free-rider problem.
- Imperfect market knowledge means consumers and producers may make economic decisions on buying and selling goods which reduce their welfare.

- Labour immobility means workers may not be allocated to their most efficient use due to geographical and occupational barriers.
- Unstable commodity markets cause dramatic fluctuations in price and revenues. This makes it difficult for consumers to budget their income and may also cause uncertainty over the availability of goods for consumption. It also makes it difficult for producers to plan their investment and ensure stability in supply from year to year.

How do governments attempt to correct market failure and what is government failure?

There are various measures a government could undertake to correct market failure: for example, indirect taxation, subsidies, tradable pollution permits, the extension of property rights, regulation, buffer stocks and minimum prices. The relative merits of each measure are now considered in relation to different types of market failure.

Indirect taxation

Indirect taxes are taxes levied on the expenditure of goods or services. The government often imposes taxes on goods which have significant external costs, such as petrol, tobacco, alcohol and electricity generated from coal-fired power stations.

Figure 29 shows the market for petrol, including both the marginal private cost curve (*MPC*) and the marginal social cost curve (*MSC*). In a free market the equilibrium price is OP_e and the equilibrium quantity OQ_e. However, the social optimum price is OP_1 and the social optimum quantity OQ_1, where marginal social cost (*MSC*) equals marginal social benefit (*MSB*) for the last unit produced. The vertical distance *ZY* represents the external cost (air pollution) for each litre of petrol consumed.

Knowledge check 40

Why are there high indirect taxes on tobacco, alcohol and petrol?

By placing a tax equal to the external cost of *ZY* per litre, the government successfully internalises the pollution. The total tax collected is shown by the area P_1YZW. Both producers and consumers pay the tax, depending on the relative elasticities of demand and supply. The consumer tax area is YP_1P_eT and the producer tax area is P_eTZW.

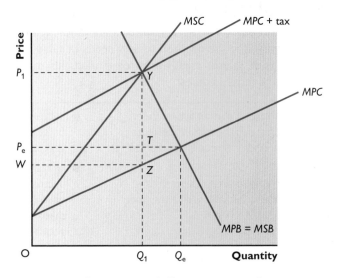

Figure 29 An indirect tax on petrol

Advantages of indirect taxes to correct market failure

- Indirect taxes are based on the principle that the polluters pay — both producer and consumer.
- Indirect taxes work with market forces, helping to internalise the external costs while maintaining consumer choice.
- The level of pollution should fall as output of the good or service is reduced and the price increased — the social optimum position of *MSB* = *MSC* can be achieved.
- Tax funds are raised for the government and these can be used to clean up the environment or to compensate the victims of pollution.

Disadvantages of indirect taxes to correct market failure

- It is difficult to quantify the pollution and then place a monetary value on it. Consequently, the social optimum position might not be achieved.
- Indirect taxes increase the costs of production for firms, making them less competitive, compared to firms in other countries where such taxes are not applied.
- Firms may relocate to other countries with less stringent taxes on production.
- The demand for the good or service may be price inelastic and so the overall reduction in pollution levels may be small.

Examiner tip

One evaluation technique is to consider the impact on different interest groups: for example, the economic effects of an increase in tax on petrol. This may have a bigger impact on consumers than petrol producers since demand is price inelastic. Petrol firms will be able to pass on most of the tax to consumers. The government is also likely to benefit from increased tax revenue.

- The tax revenue raised may not be used to compensate victims or clean up the environment.
- It might encourage the development of illegal markets: for example, tobacco and alcohol smuggling to avoid high taxes.

Subsidies

A **subsidy** is a grant provided by the government to encourage the production and consumption of a particular good or service. Subsidies are often applied on goods or services with significant external benefits, such as education and healthcare. They may also be given to alternative forms of economic activity which create less pollution, such as public transport and renewable energy.

Diagram (a) in Figure 30 shows the application of a unit subsidy to the market for electricity from renewable energy sources. The effect of a subsidy is to lower the price of each kilowatt of electricity from P_e to P_1 and increase the quantity from Q_e to Q_1.

The subsidy per unit is AB and the total subsidy area is $ABCP_1$. Part of the subsidy is passed on to consumers in the form of a lower price of electricity, equal to the area AGP_eP_1. The other portion of the subsidy ($GBCP_e$) remains with the producer. The lower price of electricity from renewable energy sources will help decrease the demand for electricity from non-renewable sources from D to D_1 (diagram (b)).

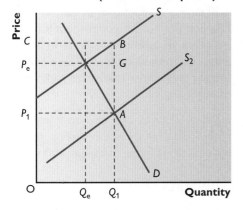
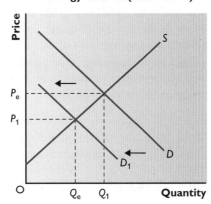

Figure 30 A unit subsidy for renewable electricity generation and the impact on the market for non-renewable electricity generation

Advantages of subsidies applied to renewable energy markets

- They reduce air pollution.
- Using renewable energy sources helps to promote sustained economic growth.
- The rate of consumption of non-renewable resources is reduced.
- Subsidies work with the market. They help to internalise the external benefits from renewable forms of energy.

Knowledge check 41

Why might a government subsidise some goods?

Examiner tip

One evaluation technique is to consider the magnitude of an event: for example, assessing the effects of government subsidies in the renewable energy markets. This will depend upon how large the subsidies are as a proportion of total production costs for firms.

Disadvantages of subsidies applied to non-renewable energy markets

- There is an opportunity cost to government subsidies. It may lead to higher taxes or cuts in government spending elsewhere.
- Firms may become inefficient in production if they rely upon subsidies.
- Wind power may be a less reliable source of energy than traditional fossil fuels.

Tradable pollution permits (carbon emissions trading)

In 2005 the European Commission set up an **emissions trading system (ETS)** in an attempt to limit greenhouse gas emissions from heavy industry. Its main focus is to curb carbon dioxide emissions by major polluters in the European Union, such as the power generators, steel, paper, cement and ceramics industries. It is intended to include the aviation industry in the scheme in 2012.

The ETS is a 'cap and trade' system. Each year, the European Commission allocates a set amount of carbon dioxide permits to national governments, which then divide up the allowances among the firms covered by the scheme. This 'caps' the amount of carbon emissions for the year. The pollution permits are **tradable**, which means that firms can buy and sell the allowances between themselves.

Most of the permits have been given free to industry and allocated on the basis of the amount of pollution created before the scheme was created. However, national governments are able to retain up to 10% of carbon permits and offer them for sale depending upon the level of scarcity. The ETS gives an incentive to firms to invest in clean technology and so reduce carbon emissions in the long term. There is also a reserve of carbon permits to enable new firms to enter those industries within the emissions trading scheme.

Knowledge check 42

What is meant by a 'cap and trade' scheme?

The ETS also allows firms to invest in schemes that reduce carbon dioxide emissions outside the European Union: for example, in India and China. The savings in carbon emissions can then be offset against their own emissions in the European Union.

Advantages of tradable pollution permits

- A market is created for buying and selling carbon permits, just like other goods and services. In effect, the price mechanism is used to internalise the external costs associated with carbon emissions.
- Pollution permits can be reduced over time as part of a coordinated plan. For example, in 2008 the European Commission cut carbon allocations by 5%.
- National governments can raise funds by selling their reserve pollution permits to industry. The revenue could then be used to clean up the environment or compensate victims.
- Firms have an incentive to invest in clean technology.
- Production costs will increase for firms that exceed their pollution allowances, since they have to purchase additional permits and this provides a source of revenue for cleaner firms that can sell their excess pollution permits.

- The ETS may act as a foundation for a global-wide scheme. It has attracted interest from developed countries outside of the EU. The North-Eastern USA has set up a parallel scheme and the state of California may create its own scheme.
- Firms are able to bank their excess pollution permits for use in future years.

Disadvantages of tradable pollution permits

- The European Commission may issue too many carbon permits so that there is little incentive for firms to reduce pollution. This occurred during the first phase of the ETS (2005–07) and led to a collapse in the price of carbon allowances. This reflected the absence of a means to bank spare allowances at the time.
- The European Commission may allocate too few carbon permits so that production costs for EU firms increase rapidly, reducing their international competitiveness. Some firms may even relocate outside of the EU to reduce production costs.
- Disputes have arisen over the allocation of carbon permits to firms. Some companies believe they should receive larger allowances and have taken legal proceedings against the European Commission.
- Firms may pass the costs of purchasing pollution permits on to their customers, leading to higher prices of, for example, electricity, steel, glass and paper. This is more likely to happen if demand is price inelastic.
- There is less pressure on major polluting firms to clean up their act if it is possible to buy extra permits from elsewhere.
- EU firms may avoid investing in expensive technology to reduce their own emissions by funding cheaper carbon offsetting schemes in developing countries.
- The price of pollution permits has fluctuated considerably since their inception in 2005. For example, the price of carbon emissions has varied from over €25 to less than €1 per ton. This has created uncertainty among firms about whether to invest heavily in carbon-reducing technology. Firms need a clear guide on what carbon prices will be for the next decade in order to determine their investment levels.
- There is a cost to the government of monitoring pollution emissions from the many companies within the scheme.
- The European Union is just one part of the world. Unless all countries engage in similar carbon trading schemes, global emissions will continue to increase. In 2007, China became the world's largest carbon polluter; however, it is currently not subject to any limits.
- The valuation of pollution permits is an inexact science. Perhaps it is too important to leave to the market. Much disagreement exists over the costs of greenhouse gas emissions. Some environmental groups believe too little is being done to reduce carbon emissions. Carbon trading is simply leading to a false sense of security.

Examiner tip
One evaluation technique is to consider both advantages and disadvantages. For example, a question on examining the advantages of tradable carbon permits as a means of reducing pollution invites you to consider the pros and cons of such a scheme.

Carbon offsetting

Carbon offsetting schemes enable consumers or producers to offset their carbon emissions by paying for the removal of the same amount of carbon emissions elsewhere. Many airlines, banks, energy and motor vehicle companies have set up carbon offsetting schemes for their own customers. For example, British Airways customers can pay an additional fee to offset the carbon produced by the flight. This is assumed to be achieved by planting trees, providing solar panels for electricity or replacing light bulbs with energy-efficient versions.

There are several limitations, one being that carbon offsetting is purely voluntary and so customers can ignore the schemes. They are also difficult to regulate and open to fraud. It is also hard to obtain an accurate measure of the emissions to be offset and the effectiveness of the schemes intended to carry this out. Finally, some of the carbon reduction schemes may have occurred irrespective of offsetting.

Renewable energy certificates

Renewable energy obligation certificates (ROCs) were introduced by the government to encourage power-generating firms to use renewable energy sources (e.g. solar, wind, tidal and wave power) to create electricity. Firms were required to have 10% of their power generation from renewable sources by 2010, rising to 15.4% by 2015.

Firms unable to meet the renewable energy target will be obliged to purchase certificates from the government, the proceeds of which are distributed to companies that do meet the target. The purchase price is set at £30 per MWh and will be adjusted in line with the retail price index. This will make renewable energy more price competitive compared to non-renewable energy sources and so promote sustainable economic growth.

Extension of property rights

This involves the government allocating property rights to organisations over the ownership of resources and regarding what uses they can be put to and what rights others have over them. An extension of property rights has been applied to the seas, rivers, mountains and air in certain areas.

Knowledge check 43

What is meant by property rights?

All too often negative externalities arise when there is a lack of property rights over a resource. There is an incentive to abuse the use of a resource if there are no property rights: for example, over-fishing in the North Sea.

Advantages of property rights

- Property rights use the market mechanism to ensure an efficient use of resources. This means the owner of the property right will charge consumers and producers for using it.
- There is an increase in the knowledge and expertise for the organisation with the property right. It takes away pressure from the government to assess the pollution.
- There is a greater likelihood that the 'property' (resources) will be managed carefully to ensure its availability for future generations, as with the control of fish catches from the North Sea.
- The property owners can charge firms that need to pollute the environment. The funds can be used to clean up the environment and compensate the sufferers.
- Firms that damage the environment without permission can be prosecuted and made to pay for clean-up operations.

Disadvantages of property rights

- It is often difficult for a government to extend property rights. For example, UK membership of the EU means that EU fishing boats are entitled to fish in UK territorial waters.

- It may be difficult for a government to extend a property right which covers more than one country. For example, the logging of the Amazonian rainforest in Brazil is outside the jurisdiction of developed countries. The external cost which arises cannot easily be internalised.
- It could be difficult to trace the source of environmental damage. In the case of asbestos sufferers who worked for more than one asbestos company, it has been extremely difficult to prove which firm caused the disease. Consequently, compensation payments have been withheld.
- The legal costs involved in prosecuting a polluter could be extremely high, deterring victims from taking action.
- It is difficult to quantify and place a monetary value on the use of a property right and so there could be an incorrect payment made for it. For example, victims of a chemical leak may not get full compensation for the damage caused.

Knowledge check 44

Why might the absence of property rights lead to market failure?

Government regulation

There are various forms of government regulation to correct market failure. In some cases direct controls are applied: for example, the Environmental Protection Act (1989) set minimum environmental standards for emissions from over 3,000 factories involved in chemical processes, waste incineration and oil refining. These firms are monitored by government pollution inspectors who have the power to impose fines and close down factories.

Advantages of regulations

- They are simple to understand: for example, legal restrictions on age limits for the sale of tobacco and alcohol.
- It is possible to fine or close down companies which have abused the regulations: for example, by emitting dangerous levels of toxic waste.
- Consumer protection laws offer some redress against firms that sell shoddy or unsafe goods, or which make false claims about their products. It may help to reduce the problem of asymmetric information.

Disadvantages of regulations

- It is expensive to monitor the behaviour of firms.
- There may be extra costs to firms: for example, the cost of installing pollution monitoring equipment.
- It may be difficult to quantify and attach a monetary value to pollution emissions.
- Regulations prevent the operation of the price mechanism, over-ruling it completely rather than working with it.
- Government failure may occur if the regulations serve to misallocate resources.

Buffer stock schemes

A buffer stock scheme may be operated by a government agency to reduce price fluctuations of a commodity and stabilise producer incomes. It involves the agency setting a target price range for a commodity (a maximum and minimum price) and then intervening to ensure that the price remains within this band despite sudden changes in supply or demand. Examples are coffee, natural rubber, tin and the wool market.

Knowledge check 45

What is the purpose of a buffer stock scheme?

In times of a good harvest (an increase in supply) the price may be in danger of falling too low and so the agency buys up the excess supply of the commodity, adding to its stockpile. In times of a poor harvest (a decrease in supply) the price may be in danger of rising too high and so the agency sells from its stockpile.

Part (a) of Figure 31 shows the operation of a buffer stock scheme for cocoa. The initial equilibrium price P_e is within the price range of P_5 and P_3. However, a very good harvest in one year increases supply to Q_1 which causes the price to fall to P_1. The agency intervenes by purchasing quantity XY which prevents the price from falling below the minimum target price P_3. Total agency spending is shown by the area XYQ_1L. It has increased its stockpile of cocoa.

Part (b) shows a poor harvest in another year which decreases supply to Q_6, putting pressure on price to rise to P_6. The agency intervenes by selling quantity VW from its stockpile which prevents price from rising above the maximum target price P_5. Total agency revenue is shown by the area $VWMQ_6$. It has reduced its stockpile of cocoa.

The scheme is meant to be self-financing, since the agency purchases stocks at a low price (P_3) and sells stock at a high price (P_5).

Knowledge check 46

Outline how a buffer stock scheme operates.

(a) **Agency purchase of stocks (a good harvest)** (b) **Agency sale of stocks (a poor harvest)**

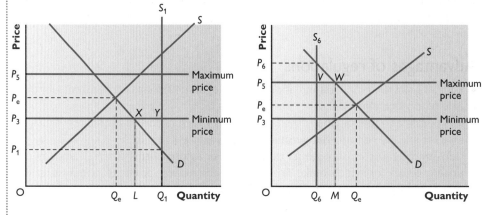

Figure 31 A buffer stock scheme for cocoa

Advantages of buffer stocks

- They reduce commodity price fluctuations, helping to stabilise producer incomes.
- There is greater certainty in the market, leading to more investment.
- They help to ensure provision of commodities for consumers even in years of poor harvests.

Disadvantages of buffer stocks

- A series of good harvests in consecutive years may put too much financial pressure on the agency that has to keep purchasing additional stocks and it may become too expensive to fund. This problem may reflect the initial setting of the price range in the first place — often at too high a level due to asymmetric information between producers and the government agency.

- The long-run trend of increased productivity in the agricultural sector creates a continuous pressure on the agency to purchase additional stocks and requires a downward adjustment of the intervention price range.
- There may be significant costs associated with the storage and security of stockpiles. Usually, large buildings are required.
- The stocks may be perishable over a long period of time, especially agricultural commodities. The agency may lose money by destroying its stocks.
- A series of poor harvests may lead to the agency running out of stocks to release to the market. This means the market price exceeds the maximum price and so the buffer stock system breaks down.

Minimum pricing

The government may stabilise commodity prices and producer incomes through a guaranteed minimum price scheme. For example, EU farmers are guaranteed a minimum price for many commodities, including sugar, wheat and barley. Usually the minimum price is set above the free-market price, causing agricultural surpluses. These are purchased by a government agency at the 'guaranteed' minimum price. This is shown in Figure 32.

A minimum price of P_2 causes demand to contract from Q_e to Q_1 and supply to extend from Q_e to Q_2. It leads to an excess supply of Q_1Q_2. Government expenditure on the surplus is shown by the area Q_1Q_2YW and total farm revenue increases from OP_eXQ_e to OP_2YQ_2. The excess supply is stockpiled by the government.

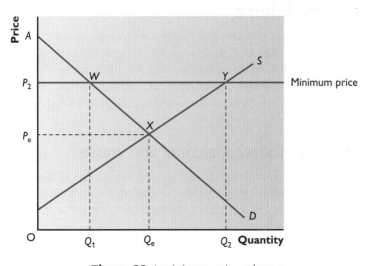

Figure 32 A minimum price scheme

Advantages of a minimum price

- A reduction of commodity price fluctuations makes it easier for consumers to budget their spending.
- Farm incomes are stabilised and increased, leading to greater investment in agriculture.

Examiner tip
One evaluation technique is to consider the possible difference between short-run and long-run effects of an event. For example, a good harvest in one year is unlikely to threaten the funding of a buffer stock scheme. However, a series of good harvests over a number of years may lead to the buffer stock agency running out of funds to purchase stock and so to the collapse of the scheme.

- Employment in the countryside is maintained, helping to reduce rural–urban inequality.
- Supply of agricultural commodities is guaranteed even in times of poor harvest, due to surplus stockpiles.
- Agricultural surpluses can be used as a form of foreign aid to developing countries.

Disadvantages of a minimum price

- The price of food increases, which could lead to hardship for consumers on low incomes.
- Government spending on agricultural surpluses involves an opportunity cost. It may have to raise taxes or cut spending on other programmes.
- There are increased storage and security costs for the food surpluses.
- The agricultural surpluses may have to be destroyed due to their perishability: for example, milk, fresh peaches and tomatoes.
- The agricultural surpluses may be sold in overseas markets at very low prices. This could damage farmers in developing countries, who are unable to compete against cheap government-owned food.
- Excess supply represents an inefficient allocation of resources.
- Farmers are guaranteed an income which might cause them to become less efficient over time. There is less incentive for farmers to improve the quality of the food or to keep production costs down. All these disadvantages are instances of government failure.

> **Examiner tip**
> Be prepared to annotate any diagrams provided in the multiple-choice questions. This includes labelling and shading in the area of government subsidy for a guaranteed minimum price diagram.

Government failure

Government failure occurs if government intervention leads to a net welfare loss. It is where the government causes a misallocation of resources in a market. However, it may be that government failure is less serious than the market failure it tries to cure, as in the case of intervention in tobacco and alcohol markets. Several types of government failure have already been discussed and it is now useful to provide some relevant examples.

High taxation on tobacco, alcohol and waste

High taxes have encouraged illegal smuggling of tobacco and alcohol into the UK. Organised crime has entered these markets, leading to smuggling on a massive scale. The government has lost a significant amount of tax revenue from these illegal activities.

The proposed tax on household waste may sound fine in theory but be unworkable in practice. Some local councils have proposed charging households an extra fee if they have more than two sacks of rubbish collected each week. This could adversely affect large families and low-income households. It could lead to an increase in fly tipping or disputes between households over the ownership of rubbish bags, especially in multi-occupancy properties.

Subsidies to bus transport

Subsidies to bus transport may not lead to a substantial rise in passenger numbers as motorists often prefer the convenience of private car journeys. In some cases, bus transport may be characterised as an inferior good. As real incomes increase, the demand for bus services will fall. This suggests that government subsidies are a waste of taxpayers' money.

Road pricing

A road congestion scheme will help reduce external costs such as traffic congestion and air and noise pollution. However, if the charge is set too high it could lead to an under-utilisation of road space. It may also be unfair to low-income motorists who cannot afford to pay the daily charge. Furthermore, it may reduce trade for businesses within the congestion charge zone. The socially optimum quantity of traffic may not be achieved.

Buffer stocks and minimum prices in agricultural markets

These schemes often lead to huge food surpluses which have to be destroyed or dumped on markets in developing countries. The government has distorted the operation of these markets, leading to an over-supply and misallocation of resources. This also represents a waste of taxpayers' money.

National minimum wage (NMW)

An NMW set above the free-market wage may lead to unemployment in certain labour markets, such as agriculture, textiles, laundry services and security work. The purpose of the NMW is to protect low-paid workers but in some cases it may increase poverty by creating unemployment.

Allocation of fish quotas

The European Commission is responsible for ensuring a sustainable level of fishing in the North Sea by allocating fish catches (quotas) for each commercial fishing boat. However, environmentalists point to depleting fish stocks and blame the government for setting fish quotas at too high a level. There are further problems of fishing boats throwing dead fish back to keep within their quotas and the poor monitoring of fish catches.

Government bureaucracy (red tape)

There are various government rules and regulations, known as 'red tape', that hinder the operation of market forces: for example, concerning proposals for constructing a third runway at Heathrow Airport. Various time-consuming planning enquiries have to be undertaken before major projects can go ahead. This could lead to under-investment in the physical infrastructure of the economy, reducing UK inward investment and UK international competitiveness. It is an example of the time lags involved in making decisions, where the government is too inflexible to respond to the needs of producers and consumers.

Summary

- The government intervenes in different ways to correct market failure, for example, indirect taxation, subsidies, tradable pollution permits, the extension of property rights, regulation, buffer stocks and minimum prices.

- Indirect taxes and tradable pollution permits are used to limit production and internalise external costs to the market.

- Government subsidies are used to increase production and internalise external benefits to the market.

- Buffer stocks and minimum price schemes are used to stabilise prices and increase producer incomes.

- Property rights schemes help establish the ownership and control of resources in order to manage their use and prevent exploitation.

- Regulations are used to support the other measures and to set limits on activities that lead to market failure.

- Government failure may occur. This is where government intervention leads to an increase in inefficiency and a net welfare loss.

- Types of government failure include: high taxes which encourage the development of illegal markets and reduce the incentive to work; subsidies which may require funding by taxes or government borrowing; minimum wage and minimum price schemes which lead to excess supply in markets; bureaucracy such as planning laws which impede the operation of market forces.

Questions & Answers

Exam format

Unit 1 comprises 50% of the weighting for the AS examination (and 25% for the A-level). In the examination you are required to answer eight supported multiple-choice questions plus one data-response question from a choice of two.

The time allowed for the examination is 1 hour and 30 minutes. There is a maximum of 80 marks; 32 marks are available in the multiple-choice section and 48 marks in the data-response section of the exam paper. This means around 35 minutes should be spent on the multiple-choice section and 50 minutes on the data-response section, leaving 5 minutes to check and amend your work.

Supported multiple-choice questions

This section contains four supported multiple-choice question papers and is designed to be a key learning, revision and exam preparation resource. You should use these questions to reinforce your understanding of the specification subject matter and as practice for completing work under test conditions.

The supported multiple-choice questions are similar in structure and style to the Unit 1 examination. However, in the examination each multiple-choice question is placed on a separate page in order to provide room for diagrams and calculations.

A maximum of 4 marks can be scored for each question. Students can gain 1 mark for selecting the correct option and 3 marks for explanation. Correct answers are given at the end of the multiple-choice section, together with mark schemes indicating how explanation marks would be awarded. If the incorrect option is selected you can still achieve up to 3 marks for a relevant explanation.

It is also possible to gain up to 3 marks by explaining why one or two or three of the alternative options are incorrect. This is a useful strategy to apply when uncertain about your explanation of the correct option or where your explanation lacks detail. However, you must state the option key being rejected.

Paper 1 The nature of economics

1 **Which of the following is a normative economic statement?**

   A The planned cuts in corporation tax rate from 28% to 23% between 2011 and 2014 is likely to increase business investment.

   B A change in the rate of income tax affects disposable income.

   C Income tax should be decreased from 50% to 40% for those earning more than £150,000 per year.

   D High rates of income tax affect the incentive to work.

2

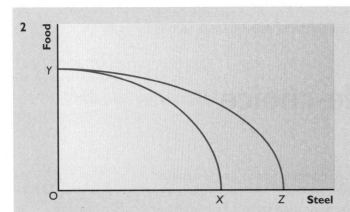

  The figure shows the production possibility frontier for a country moving from *YX* to *YZ*. The most likely cause of this is:

  A An increase in demand for steel

  B A shift of resources from food to steel production

  C Technological improvements in the steel industry

  D Exhaustion of iron ore deposits used to produce steel

3 **Which of the following statements concerning opportunity cost is correct?**

  A It is always measured in money terms.

  B It occurs in market economies but not mixed economies.

  C It indicates that resources are infinite.

  D It occurs for both consumers and producers.

4 A fast food restaurant carries out labour specialisation in the production of burgers. The purpose of this is to:

A Achieve benefits from the division of labour

B Increase the total costs of production

C Achieve benefits from economies of scale

D Increase employment for those who want a job

5 A free-market economy differs from a mixed economy in the following way:

A Business is organised to produce necessities rather than luxuries.

B All resources are allocated by the price mechanism.

C Essential services such as healthcare and education are provided free to all and funded from taxation.

D Most resources are owned and controlled by the government.

6 The problem of scarcity could be reduced by:

A Increasing the consumption of energy

B Giving everyone more money

C Government intervention to fix the price of goods

D The discovery of more resources

7 Which of the following is a positive economic statement?

A There is an opportunity cost to increasing government spending on defence.

B Increasing university tuition fees is fair.

C The provision of public goods should be left to market forces.

D A private healthcare system works better than the National Health Service.

8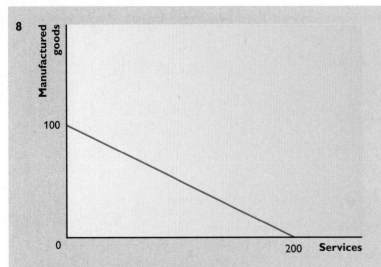

The diagram above shows a production possibility frontier for a country. Which of the following statements is true?

A The output of manufactured goods will equal the output of services.

B The opportunity cost of one extra unit of manufactured good increases as output increases.

C There is a constant rate of consumer demand for both manufactured goods and services.

D There is a constant rate of opportunity cost between manufactured goods and services.

Paper 2 **The demand for goods and services**

I **Which of the following will cause an increase in the price of steel without shifting its supply curve?**

A An increase in indirect tax on steel

B An increase in the price of iron ore, the raw material used to produce steel

C The withdrawal of a subsidy for steel producers

D An increase in the price of steel substitutes, such as aluminium and tin

2

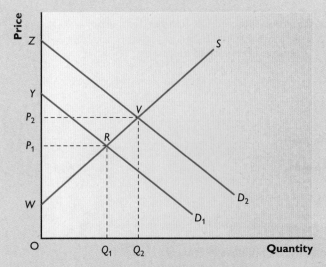

The diagram above shows the market for wheat. A shift in the demand curve for wheat from D_1 to D_2 will cause:

A An increase in total revenue

B A decrease in producer surplus

C A decrease in demand for wheat

D A decrease in consumer surplus

3 The owner of a cinema decides to reduce the price of each ticket from £6 to £3. This causes ticket sales to increase for each showing from 200 to 400.

The best estimate for price elasticity of demand is:

A −0.5

B −1.0

C −1.5

D −2.0

4 The table shows the income elasticities of demand for selected **UK** holiday destinations.

Holiday destination	Income elasticity of demand
Bournemouth	2.0
Newquay	0.6
Margate	−0.4

It may be deduced from the data in the table that:

A All the holiday destinations are normal goods.

B Holidays in Bournemouth are price elastic in demand.

C A decrease in real income will cause a decrease in demand for holidays in Newquay.

D There is a negative cross elasticity of demand for holidays in Margate.

5 If the price elasticity of demand for coffee is −0.4 and the cross elasticity of demand between tea and coffee is +0.5, a 10% decrease in the price of coffee will cause:

A A 4% fall in demand for coffee and the demand for tea to rise by 5%

B A 4% rise in demand for coffee and the demand for tea to fall by 5%

C A 40% rise in demand for coffee and the demand for tea to fall by 50%

D A 0.4% fall in demand for coffee and the demand for tea to rise by 0.5%

6 The following table shows the demand and supply schedules for a good. (You may use the blank column in your explanation).

Price per unit (£)	Quantity demanded (units)	Quantity supplied (units)	New quantity demanded (units)
10	200	1,800	
9	400	1,600	
8	600	1,400	
7	800	1,200	
6	1,000	1,000	
5	1,200	800	
4	1,400	600	

An increase in demand of 400 units at every price level will cause:

A An increase in the equilibrium price but not quantity

B An increase in the equilibrium quantity but not price

C An increase in the equilibrium price and quantity

D Equilibrium price and quantity to remain constant

7 The demand for petrol is price inelastic. Other things being equal, an increase in the price of petrol will:

A Decrease total consumer spending on petrol

B Increase demand for motor vehicles

C Increase total revenue for petrol companies

D Decrease costs of production for road haulage companies

8 Assuming there are normal demand and supply curves for a good, an increase in consumer demand is likely to:

A Decrease consumer surplus

B Discourage new firms from entering the market

C Decrease market price

D Increase producer surplus

Paper 3 The supply of goods and services

I   Which of the following will cause the price of strawberries to fall without a shift in the demand curve?

A   An increase in the price of fresh cream, a complement to strawberries

B   A decrease in the productivity of strawberry farm workers

C   An increase in the price of cherries, a substitute for strawberries

D   A decrease in the wages of strawberry farm workers

2

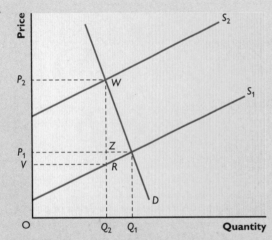

The diagram shows a tax placed on tobacco which shifts the supply curve from S_1 to S_2. Which of the following is correct about the nature and incidence of the tax?

A   It is *ad valorem*, the incidence falling mainly on tobacco producers.

B   It is specific, the incidence falling mainly on tobacco consumers.

C   It is *ad valorem*, the incidence falling mainly on tobacco consumers.

D   It is specific, the incidence falling mainly on tobacco producers.

3   Good **X** has a very low price elasticity of supply. **Which of the following is most likely to be good X?**

A   A newspaper, because it forms a relatively insignificant part of the total expenditure of a household

B   Toothpaste, because it has no close substitutes

C   Fresh tomatoes, since they are a perishable agricultural good

D   Alcohol, because it is an addictive good

4

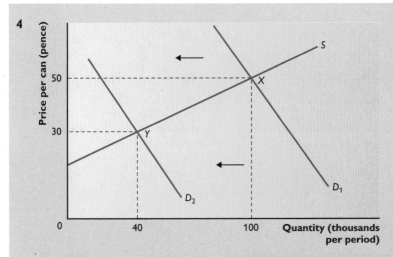

The diagram shows the demand and supply curves for a local fizzy drinks firm. The equilibrium position is initially **X** but, following a decrease in demand from D_1 to D_2 and a fall in market price, the firm intends to reduce production to point **Y**. The best estimate for price elasticity of supply is:

A   1.5

B   −0.66

C   −1.5

D   0.66

5

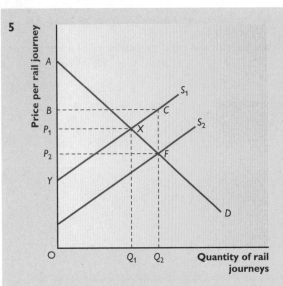

The diagram shows a unit subsidy placed on rail travel between London and Bath, shifting the supply curve from S_1 to S_2. Which of the following is correct?

A Consumer surplus increases by P_1P_2FX.

B The total subsidy area is OP_2FQ_2.

C Producer surplus increases to P_1XY.

D The rail fare falls by the same amount as the unit subsidy.

6 Which of the following will cause the price of diamonds to rise without shifting the demand curve?

A Discovery of new diamond resources in South Africa

B A decrease in the price of platinum jewellery

C The diamond company De Beers reducing its stockpile of diamonds

D An increase in mining costs for extracting diamonds

7

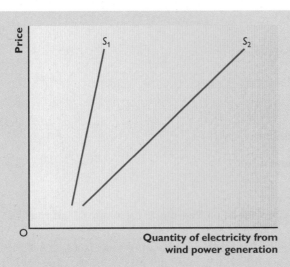

The diagram shows how the price elasticity of supply of electricity from wind power generation may vary over time. Which of the following is most likely to be true?

A Price elasticity of supply is unitary along each supply curve.

B S_1 is likely to be the short-run supply curve and S_2 the long-run supply curve.

C Price elasticity of supply remains constant along each supply curve.

D S_1 is perfectly price inelastic in supply and S_2 perfectly price elastic in supply.

8 The table shows the demand and supply schedules for a luxury range of caviar. (You may use the blank column for your explanation).

Price per unit (£)	Quantity demanded (boxes)	Quantity supplied (boxes)	New quantity supplied (boxes)
50	120	240	
40	140	220	
30	160	200	
20	180	180	
10	200	160	

If the government introduces an indirect tax of £20 per box of caviar, the tax revenue obtained will be:

A £4,400

B £3,600

C £3,200

D £2,800

Paper 4 Market failure and government failure

1   All of the following are examples of market failure *except*:

   A   External costs and benefits

   B   Under-provision of public goods

   C   Geographical and occupational immobility of labour

   D   Unemployment created by the national minimum wage

2   A flood defence scheme for London is *unlikely* to be provided in a free-market economy. This may be because of:

   A   A shortage of drinking water

   B   The free rider problem

   C   The ability to charge households for their individual consumption

   D   A lack of technology for constructing the flood barrier

3   The table shows the demand and supply schedules for barley, an agricultural good.

Price (£)	Quantity demanded (million tons)	Quantity supplied (million tons)
140	20	24
120	21	23
100	22	22
80	23	21
60	24	20

   A government agency introduces a guaranteed minimum price at £120 per ton, leading to:

   A   An increase in government agency spending

   B   A decrease in price

   C   An excess demand

   D   A decrease in supply

4 A negative externality exists when:

  A The consumption of a product provides benefits to third parties

  B The social cost exceeds the private cost in production

  C Costs are internalised by the price mechanism

  D The social cost is less than the private cost in consumption

5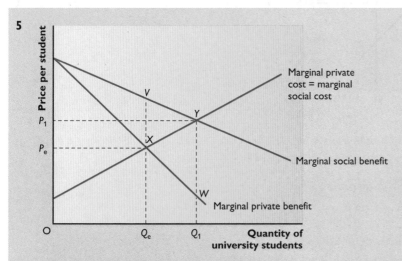

The diagram shows the market for university education. Assume there are no external costs and no government intervention. Which of the following is correct?

  A There is an over-consumption of university education.

  B Private benefits exceed social benefits.

  C Welfare can be increased by raising the quantity of students from Q_e to Q_1.

  D External benefits exceed social benefits.

6

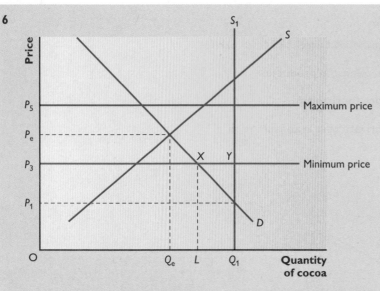

The diagram shows the operation of a buffer stock scheme for cocoa by an agency. Following a good harvest, supply increases to S_1 for a given year. The agency will:

A Allow the market price of cocoa to increase to P_5

B Reduce its stockpile of cocoa

C Allow the market price of cocoa to decrease to P_1

D Add to its stockpile of cocoa

7 Tradable pollution permits may be ineffective in reducing carbon dioxide emissions within the European Union if:

A Firms find it difficult to relocate production outside of the EU

B There is an excess demand for pollution permits

C It is easy to monitor carbon emissions from firms

D Supply exceeds demand for pollution permits

8 There may be under-consumption of fruit and vegetables in a free market due to:

A Symmetrical information between producers and consumers

B A government subsidy to fruit and vegetable producers

C Imperfect market information

D The market output exceeding the social optimum output

Answers to multiple-choice papers

Up to 3 explanation marks can be gained by rejecting 3 incorrect options as long as different reasons are given.

Paper 1

Question 1

Correct answer C. (1 mark)

Definition of normative statement. (1 mark)

Includes the term 'should' and so is normative. (1 mark)

The others are positive statements and so are based on asserting facts. (1 mark)

Question 2

Correct answer C. (1 mark)

Definition of production possibility frontier. (1 mark)

The potential output of steel has increased. (1 mark)

New technology could lead to more efficient machinery and plant. (1 mark)

Question 3

Correct answer D. (1 mark)

Definition of opportunity cost. (1 mark)

Application to consumer (for example, £10 spent on burger meal means forgoing spending £10 on a new scarf). (1 mark)

Application to producer (for example, investing £1m on new machinery means £1m less funds for shareholder dividends). (1 mark)

Question 4

Correct answer A. (1 mark)

Definition of division of labour. (1 mark)

Application and explanation of two benefits of division of labour for burger restaurant (for example, shorter training period per task, more efficient use of tills and deep fat fryers or that repetition increases expertise and so raises productivity). (1 + 1 marks)

Question 5

Correct answer B. (1 mark)

Definition of free-market economy other than that offered in correct option (for example, demand and supply determine resource allocation with no government intervention). (1 mark)

Application (for example, the price mechanism would provide all education and healthcare services). (1 mark)

Identify a mixed economy as one with both a public and private sector. (1 mark)

Question 6

Correct answer D. (1 mark)

Definition of scarcity. (1 mark)

Application and explanation of discovery of new resources (for example, vast new deposits of oil and gas discovered in the Falklands could help alleviate shortage of energy for production of goods and services). (1 + 1 marks)

Question 7

Correct answer A. (1 mark)

Definition of positive statement. (1 mark)

Application to opportunity cost (for example, increased defence spending might mean less funds available for education). (1 mark)

The others are normative statements and so are based on value judgements. (1 mark)

Question 8

Correct answer D. (1 mark)

Definition of production possibility frontier or opportunity cost. (1 mark)

Application and explanation of constant opportunity cost, since gradient is constant. (1 mark)

One manufactured good costs the output of two services. (1 mark)

Paper 2

Question 1

Correct answer D. (1 mark)

An increase in the price of tin and aluminium will cause an increase in demand for substitutes such as steel. (1 mark)

Other things being equal, an increase in demand for steel will push up the price. (1 mark)

Application with demand and supply diagram. (1 mark)

Also accept positive cross elasticity of demand discussion. (1 mark)

Question 2

Correct answer A. (1 mark)

Definition of total revenue. (1 mark)

Original total revenue OP_1RQ_1. (1 mark)

New total revenue OP_2VQ_2. (1 mark)

Question 3

Correct answer D. (1 mark)

Definition or formula of PED. (1 mark)

Workings of calculation ($+100\% \div -50\% = -2$). (1 + 1 marks)

Question 4

Correct answer C. (1 mark)

Definition or formula of YED. (1 mark)

Holidays to Newquay are a normal good with a positive YED. (1 mark)

Application (for example, a 10% fall in income causes a 6% fall in demand for holidays in Newquay). (1 mark)

Also accept holidays to Newquay are income inelastic in demand since it is less than 1. (1 mark)

Question 5

Correct answer B. (1 mark)

Definition or formula for PED or XED. (1 mark)

Workings of calculations (for example, +4% ÷ -10% = -0.4 for coffee). (1 mark)

Calculation of -5% ÷ -10% = 0.5 for tea. (1 mark)

Also accept that tea and coffee are substitutes with a positive XED. (1 mark)

Question 6

Correct answer C. (1 mark)

Original equilibrium price is £6 and quantity 1,000. (1 mark)

New equilibrium price rises to £7 and quantity to 1,200. (1 + 1 marks)

This may be shown by completion of blank column provided.

Question 7

Correct answer C. (1 mark)

Definition or formula of PED. (1 mark)

Explanation of rise in total revenue (for example, percentage rise in price is greater than percentage fall in demand). (1 mark)

Diagram showing an increase in total revenue. (1 mark)

Question 8

Correct answer D. (1 mark)

Definition of producer surplus. (1 mark)

Application and explanation by diagram showing an increase in demand with original and new levels of producer surplus. (1 + 1 marks).

Paper 3

Question 1

Correct answer D. (1 mark)

A decrease in wages will lower the unit cost of strawberries. (1 mark)

This increases the supply curve. (1 mark)

The result is a reduction of the price. (1 mark)

Also marks available for a diagram showing an increase in supply and a decrease in price. (1 + 1 marks)

Question 2

Correct answer B. (1 mark)

Definition of specific tax. (1 mark)

Consumers pay tax area P_1P_2WZ. (1 mark)

Producers pay tax area P_1ZRV. (1 mark)

A mark for the idea of specific tax since it is a parallel shift in supply curve. (1 mark)

Producers pay most of the tax since demand is price elastic. (1 mark)

Question 3

Correct answer C. (1 mark)

Definition or formula of PES. (1 mark)

Explanation and application of low PES for fresh tomatoes (for example, cannot be stored, so no spare stocks and long time period needed to grow). (1 + 1 marks)

Explanation of low PES in terms of inelastic supply. (1 mark)

Question 4

Correct answer A. (1 mark)

Definition or formula of PES. (1 mark)

Workings of calculation (-60% ÷ -40% = 1.5). (1 + 1 marks)

Explanation that supply is price elastic. (1 mark)

Question 5

Correct answer A. (1 mark)

Definition of consumer surplus. (1 mark)

Original consumer surplus is AXP_1. (1 mark)

The new level of consumer surplus is AFP_2. (1 mark)

Question 6

Correct answer D. (1 mark)

Increase in mining costs means higher production costs. (1 mark)

Supply shifts vertically upwards. (1 mark)

This causes an increase in price. (1 mark)

A diagram showing a decrease in supply and an increase in price. (1 + 1 marks)

Question 7

Correct answer B. (1 mark)

Definition or formula of PES. (1 mark)

S_1 is short-run supply where at least one factor input is fixed, so supply cannot easily respond to a rising price. (1 mark)

S_2 is long-run supply where all factor inputs are variable, so supply can respond more easily to a rise in price. (1 mark)

Application to wind power (takes time to gain planning permission and construct more wind turbines). (1 mark)

Question 8

Correct answer C. (1 mark)

Definition of indirect tax. (1 mark)

Workings of calculation ($160 \times £20 = £3,200$). (1 + 1 marks)

Identifying the new equilibrium price of £30. (1 mark)

Paper 4

Question 1

Correct answer D. (1 mark)

Definition of government failure. (1 mark)

Explanation of NMW leading to a contraction in demand and extension in supply of labour, creating unemployment. (1 + 1 marks)

Diagrammatic analysis. (1 + 1 marks)

Question 2

Correct answer B. (1 mark)

Definition of a public good. (1 mark)

Explanation and application of the free rider problem to a flood defence scheme. (1 + 1 marks)

Question 3

Correct answer A. (1 mark)

Definition of a guaranteed minimum price. (1 mark)

Excess supply is created which government has to purchase to ensure scheme remains in operation. (1 mark)

Calculation of government spending on the scheme ($£120 \times 2$ million tons = £240 million). (2 marks)

Question 4

Correct answer B. (1 mark)

Definition of a negative externality. (1 mark) A relevant diagram. (1 mark)

Explanation that social costs include both private and external costs. (1 mark)

Application to an example of an external cost (such as pollution). (1 mark)

Question 5

Correct answer C. (1 mark)

Definition of welfare gain (social benefit exceeds social cost). (1 mark)

Application and explanation to increase quantity by Q_eQ_1 (for example, social benefit Q_eQ_1YV exceeds social cost Q_eQ_1YX). (1 + 1 marks)

Question 6

Correct answer D. (1 mark)

Definition of buffer stocks scheme. (1 mark)

Agency will purchase XY or LQ_1 of cocoa at the minimum price P_3. (1 + 1 marks)

The total area of agency spending is equal to XYQ_1L. (1 mark)

Question 7

Correct answer D. (1 mark)

Definition of tradable pollution permit. (1 mark)

If supply exceeds demand, there is a downward pressure on the price of tradable permits. (1 mark)

There is less incentive for firms to cut back on pollution. (1 mark)

Total supply could exceed demand, causing price to fall to zero. (1 mark)

Question 8

Correct answer C. (1 mark)

Imperfect market information is a market failure leading to an inefficient allocation of resources. (1 mark)

Explanation of imperfect market information. (1 mark)

Consumers may have fewer fruit and vegetables than is required for a healthy diet. (1 mark)

Data-response questions

Evaluation in data-response questions

The data-response exam paper is typically marked in two parts by examiners: first, for knowledge, application and analysis marks (KAA); and second, for evaluation marks. There are 32 marks for KAA and 16 marks for evaluation. Evaluation marks are only available in the data-response paper, usually for the higher-mark base questions. Three of the five sub-questions include evaluation marks.

The command words used for evaluation are: *examine, evaluate, assess, discuss, comment upon* and *to what extent*. Any of these words in the question indicate that you should demonstrate some critical understanding of the issues being discussed.

Question 1 **The housing market in England**

Table 1 Average house price, annual earnings and unemployment rate by region, 2011

Region	Average property price	Average earnings	Unemployment rate (% of workforce unemployed)
North West	£150,315	£23,886	7.5%
Yorks & Humber	£121,844	£23,138	9.3%
North East	£107,011	£22,666	10.2%
East Midlands	£125,444	£23,789	8.0%
West Midlands	£133,295	£23,465	9.8%
East England	£174,550	£25,337	6.6%
South West	£175,995	£23,499	6.1%
South East	£208,292	£27,499	6.1%
Greater London	£341,871	£40,500	9.0%
England	£162,379	£25,948	8.0%

Source: **www.ONS.org.uk**

Extract I

Falling house prices in England

House prices have fallen by more than 30% since their peak in 2007 and are set to fall a further 10% by 2012 as banks remain cautious on issuing mortgage loans (house loans) and demand higher cash deposits from borrowers. House prices have also been affected by the sluggish state of the economy, falling consumer confidence and rising unemployment as government spending cuts take hold. In such an economic climate, most building firms have cut back on new housing projects and reduced their staff.

Falling house prices should be good news for first-time buyers. However, the uncertainty over job security and the reluctance of banks to lend has prevented many from getting on to the property ladder. Often these are young and dynamic workers, essential for wealth creation. In normal circumstances, people can borrow up to three times their annual income for a mortgage; but this is nowhere near enough for first-time buyers, who tend to be in the early stages of their careers.

Regional house price differences remain. This has led to shortages of skilled workers in Greater London, especially in the nursing, teaching and fire fighter professions. Geographical immobility of labour threatens economic recovery. However, in less skilled occupations, net migration to the UK over recent years has helped prevent labour shortages. Also, rising unemployment from government spending cuts and low economic growth suggest there is plenty of spare labour available across the country to fill job vacancies. In March 2011 the government Office for National Statistics estimated there to be 501,000 job vacancies and 2,500,000 unemployed.

(a) With reference to Extract 1, explain the causes of the fall in house prices since 2007. Use a demand and supply diagram in your answer. (6 marks)

ⓔ You should refer to the causes mentioned in the extract and ensure that a diagram is offered. If no diagram is provided then the maximum marks awarded will be capped — usually at 3.

(b) Explain the likely economic effects of falling house prices on the demand and wage rates for building workers. (4 marks)

ⓔ Try to consider the key concept underlying the question: namely, derived demand.

(c) Discuss the possible economic effects of falling house prices on first-time buyers. (10 marks)

ⓔ A discussion can include both positive and negative effects and will require a conclusion at the end. Be prepared to offer two evaluation points for 10 mark-base questions.

(d) With reference to Extract 1 and Table 1, select two regions and examine two possible reasons why average house prices differ between them. (14 marks)

ⓔ Follow the instructions and stick with a comparison of just two regions. Choose extremes when contrasting as it is easier to discuss the differences. Be prepared to offer up to three evaluation points for 14 mark-base questions.

(e) To what extent might regional house price differences cause market failure? (14 marks)

ⓔ The command phrase 'To what extent' invites you to consider the degree to which you agree with the statement, supporting your argument with evidence. Be prepared to qualify your answer so you that might not fully agree, or even consider ways around the problem of market failure.

Student answer

(a) House prices have fallen by more than 30% since 2007 as a result of the credit crunch where banks have been hit by people not repaying their loans. **a** The banks have made it much harder for people to obtain a mortgage due to fear of more debt defaults. Also, there is very low consumer confidence and rising unemployment. In such an environment people are unlikely to buy houses. **b** Consequently, demand for housing has fallen from D to D_1, causing prices to fall from P_e to P_1.

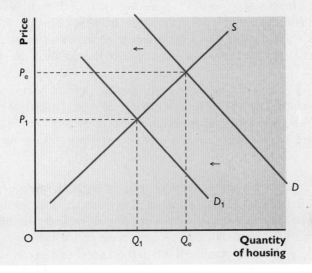

ⓔ **6/6 marks. a** The student explicitly refers to the fall in house prices (1 mark). **b** Two reasons are given for the fall in house prices (1+1 marks). **c** A correct diagram is drawn and briefly explained (3 marks).

(b) The decrease in demand for houses will cause a decrease in demand for building workers. **a** This is because labour is a derived demand — it is not wanted for its own sake but rather for what it produces. **b** The fall in demand for houses has led to reduction in house prices. Building firms will also reduce wages to cut their costs of production and restore some of their profits. **c**

ⓔ **4/4 marks. a** The student identifies that the demand for labour will fall (1 mark). **b** A definition of derived demand and its application is provided (1+1 marks). **c** The wage rate for building workers will fall (1 mark). The student answers the question directly.

(c) The 30% decrease in house prices should be good news for first-time buyers since it means housing becomes more affordable. **a** However, property buyers are usually limited to borrowing up to three times their annual income and so it depends on whether house prices will fall enough or incomes rise fast enough. Unfortunately we can see that the ratio of house prices to average earnings in England is more than 6 to 1 (£162,379 ÷ £25,948) and so first-time buyers are unlikely to be able to borrow enough. Also, rising unemployment and pay freezes

for public sector workers mean that incomes are not rising. Even a further fall in house prices by 10% in 2012 will be of little help.

Moreover, many first-time buyers are at an early stage of their career and so presumably they have not reached their maximum earnings potential. This could make it really hard to buy a property, especially when interest rates are likely to rise which will increase the monthly mortgage repayment. **b**

On the other hand, the house-price data shown in Table 1 is only an average. There must be cheaper properties in each region — for example, one-bedroom flats and apartments or properties in run down areas. Perhaps first-time buyers need to consider these properties to get on the housing ladder and to move northwards where they are typically cheaper. In conclusion, it may depend on the willingness of first-time buyers to compromise on the quality of the property. **c**

ⓔ **10/10 marks. a** Housing should become more affordable for first-time buyers (1 mark). **b** But problems exist, such as the high house price–earnings ratio and (3 marks) the poor state of the economy and relatively low incomes due to early part of career (1 + 1 marks). Good use of the figures is made. **c** Two evaluation points are given, such as buying cheaper small homes in run down areas and the possibility of moving northwards (2 + 2 marks).

(d) Large differences in regional house prices exist in England. Average house prices in Greater London (£341,871) are 3.1 times more expensive than for the North East (£107,011). **a** This is a really big difference and probably reflects the differences in regional income and wealth. On average, people earn a higher income in Greater London (£40,500) than the North East (£22,666) and so can afford to take out bigger mortgages and pay more for houses. The ratio of average earnings between Greater London and the North is 1.8 to 1. Also there is a lot of wealth built up in houses over many years in Greater London. When people move homes in Greater London they probably have a lot of wealth in the house to take with them to put as a deposit on their new home.

A second reason might be due to the greater scarcity of land for building on in Greater London compared to the North. There are very tight planning restrictions in Greater London since it is already a big urban area and so not much land becomes available to build on. This means demand will tend to exceed supply, pushing up the price of land. In the North there is more land available to build on so the price of this is lower, reducing the costs of building houses. This will lead to lower house prices.

The higher level of demand compared to supply between the two regions is shown in the diagram. The house price equilibrium is much higher in Greater London. **b**

Both of the reasons given are very important causes of regional house price differences. I think differences in income and wealth are the most significant since it will determine how much people can borrow and spend on buying a house, especially as the government has relaxed planning laws to encourage the provision of more building land. One could note that there are other possible factors that help explain regional house price differences, such as unemployment rates, job vacancies, investment levels and the cost of living.

However, the unemployment rates for Greater London (9.0%) and the North East (10.2%) are very similar, which suggests this is not a cause of house price differences.

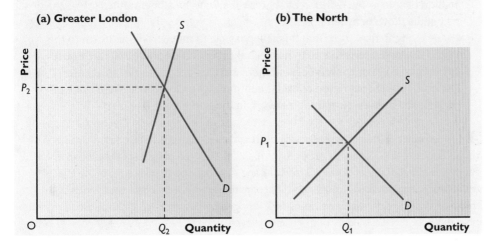

(a) Greater London

(b) The North

@ 14/14 marks. a Explicit use of house price data (1 mark). b Two possible causes of regional house price differences identified (1 + 1 marks) and both explained by reference and manipulation of the data from the table. Diagrammatic analysis is also used to back up one of the reasons (3 + 3 marks). Note that a maximum of 8 knowledge, application and analysis marks is available. c Evaluation is offered by prioritising between the two causes (2 marks) and opening up the possibility of further determinants of regional differences (2 marks). The argument that both regions have similar unemployment rates helps to reject unemployment as a possible cause (2 marks).

(e) Market failure is when the price mechanism fails to allocate resources efficiently and so leads to a net welfare loss. a Regional house price differences on such a large scale can cause a market failure. This is because it leads to a geographical immobility of labour — where labour from the northern regions cannot afford to move to Greater London and take up work since they cannot pay for more expensive housing costs. b It means there are unemployed resources and so the economy operates within its production possibility frontier. Workers are simply priced out of the housing markets in the South East. This is sometimes called the North–South divide. c Note the staff shortages that exist in fire fighting, nursing and teaching in Greater London, which reduce the quality of services provided. In the long term, it could seriously reduce the quality of human capital, leading to lower productivity and competitiveness. Firms might find they cannot fill job vacancies and cut back on expansion plans or even leave the region. It is interesting to note that there are 0.5 million job vacancies which need to be filled and 2.5 million unemployed. This implies the existence of labour immobility (though it includes both geographical and occupational types).

However, the extract refers to the large-scale immigration into the UK over recent years, probably following the expansion of the European Union in 2004. This has helped reduce the shortage of labour in Greater London and elsewhere. Indeed, unemployment has been rising and is at 9% in Greater London,

suggesting plentiful supply of workers. Also, it indicates that the problem of regional house price differences can be partly overcome through market forces of labour migration to the UK. The UK is a dynamic economy with more than 30 million people in the workforce. There will always be some unfilled job vacancies as people move between posts.

One might also argue that it is still possible to move from the North to the South if people are prepared to have smaller properties. Moreover, the house price figures are only averages and there are cheaper properties in Greater London. People could even consider commuting to work since there is a well-established motorway and rail network in the South East. **d**

e **14/14 marks. a** The student starts by defining the key concept in the question: namely, 'market failure' — this is always a good idea (1 mark). **b** The type of market failure is explained (geographical immobility of labour) (2 marks) **c** and developed further in terms of the effects on the production possibility frontier and UK competitiveness — with data use (5 marks). **d** Evaluation marks are gained by discussing how immigration has alleviated the problem (2 marks) and stating that there are plenty of spare unemployed workers even in Greater London (2 marks); furthermore, people can always downsize their homes when moving south or commute longer distances to work via the transport network (2 marks).

Total score: 48/48 = a top grade A

Question 2 **The oil and petrol markets**

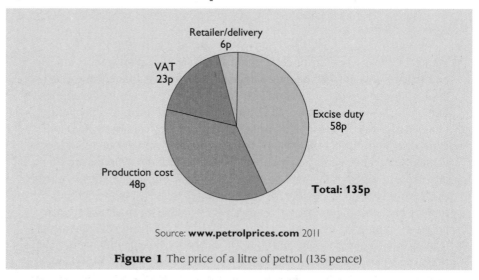

Source: **www.petrolprices.com** 2011

Figure 1 The price of a litre of petrol (135 pence)

Extract 1

Soaring oil and petrol prices

Oil prices have soared over the past 7 years from $25 a barrel in 2004 to $125 in 2011. Industrialisation of China and India has led to growing oil consumption. Indeed, China is now the world's largest importer of oil, sucking in 10 million barrels a day.

Instability in the Middle East — a major oil-producing region — has also led to disruption in supply. To make matters worse, the oil cartel OPEC (Organisation of Petroleum Exporting Countries) has reduced production in order to increase its revenues.

At $125 a barrel, oil is directing huge sums of money from consumers to producers, mainly in the Middle East. Oil exports from this region are now worth $850 billion a year. The oil-producing countries have so much cash that they are buying Western assets. These investments are estimated to exceed $10,000 billion according to the International Monetary Fund.

Rising oil prices have caused a knock-on effect in other markets. The price of petrol (which is made from refining oil) has risen over the past 7 years in the UK, from £0.80 per litre in 2004 to £1.35 in 2011.

However, technology may come to the rescue as alternative sources of energy are developed. The government has provided more than £500 million in subsidies to the construction of wind and wave power farms over recent years. Motor vehicles are also becoming more fuel efficient and there has been a rush to develop biofuels. These use cereals to produce oil for motor vehicles. Electric-powered cars are also becoming more fashionable in urban areas. This may help reduce the dependency on oil.

(a) Using a supply and demand diagram, outline why 'oil prices have soared over the past 7 years'. (6 marks)

ⓔ It is good practice to show both the outward shift in the demand curve and the inward shift in the supply curve on the same diagram. Make sure you label the original and final equilibrium price and quantity positions.

(b) With reference to Figure 1, explain why oil prices have risen at a faster rate than petrol prices. (4 marks)

ⓔ Make sure you refer to the data in Figure 1 in your answer. There are usually one or two data marks available in such questions.

(c) Discuss how the price elasticity of demand for oil might change over time. (10 marks)

ⓔ This question requires reference to 'time'. It is a good idea to divide up into the short-run and long-run implications as this offers a means to evaluate.

(d) Examine the likely economic effects of an increase in indirect taxation on the market for petrol. Use a supply and demand diagram in your answer. (14 marks)

ⓔ Make sure the diagram is correctly labelled and explained since up to 5 marks are usually available. The term 'examine' requires you to consider both the positive and negative effects of the increase in tax and come to some conclusion about its desirability.

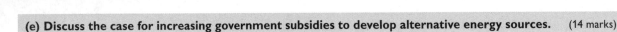
(e) Discuss the case for increasing government subsidies to develop alternative energy sources. (14 marks)

ⓔ Although the question does not require a diagram, be prepared to offer one that will enhance your answer (namely a subsidy diagram). Diagrammatic analysis demonstrates an understanding of the price mechanism model which is at the centre of Unit 1. To evaluate, consider the limitations of the 'case for increasing subsidies': in other words, the case against. It is a simple but effective way to gain evaluation marks.

Student answer

(a) The price of oil has soared over the past 7 years due to instability in the Middle East and OPEC's decision to reduce production, which have caused supply to decrease. **a** The supply curve shifts inwards from S_1 to S_2 and so raises the price from P_1 to P_2 in the diagram. **b**

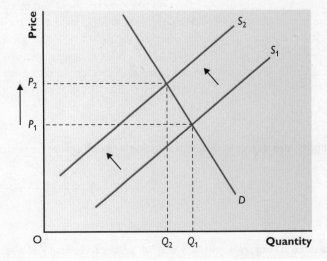

ⓔ **3/6 marks. a** The student identifies reasons for a decrease in supply causing oil prices to rise (1 mark). **b** The supply curve is shifted correctly, showing the original and new equilibrium positions (2 marks). However, the student fails to see that demand for oil has increased due to industrialisation of China and India — so the demand curve should shift too, leading to a higher price. Identifying the increase in demand and adding this to the diagram would ensure full marks. Another way of gaining a mark would be to state the actual increase in oil price from $25 to $125 a barrel over the period. This is something that students often forget to do.

(b) Oil prices have risen faster than petrol prices. This is due to oil being just one input which goes into making petrol. **a** There are other costs to consider such as refining the oil, machinery and labour costs of processing it into petrol. Consequently, large increases in oil prices will lead to relatively lower increases in petrol prices. **b**

ⓔ **3/4 marks. a** The student explains that oil is just one input involved in producing petrol (1 mark) and then **b** gives examples of other input costs (2 marks). No data reference is provided: for example, estimating the percentage increases in oil prices (400%) and petrol prices (69%) would gain another mark. Also, the student should refer to Figure 1, which shows that 60% of the price of petrol is actually tax (81 pence from 135 pence). This would secure another mark. A cap on marks is usually set if students do not make use of the data as instructed in the question.

(c) Price elasticity of demand refers to the responsiveness of demand for a good due to a change in its price. **a** There are several key determinants of a good, such as whether it is a luxury or necessity, the proportion of income spent on it and whether there are close substitutes. Oil is regarded as an essential good with no close substitutes and so demand is likely to be inelastic. **b** This means the percentage change in demand is less than the percentage change in price. A rise in price of oil will increase revenue to oil producers and this is implied in the extract as the reason for OPEC reducing supply. **c** The use of oil is also habit forming since we drive our cars all the time, so demand will remain inelastic. **d**

ⓔ 6/10 marks. a The student defines price elasticity of demand (1 mark) and **b** explains some important determinants, applying to oil (2 marks). **c** It is suggested that oil is price inelastic in demand and this is explained by reference to the reason for OPEC restricting supply to gain more revenue (2 marks). **d** The student's final sentence provides another reason for oil being price inelastic in demand (1 mark). All 6 KAA marks are gained. However, no evaluation marks are awarded as there is little attempt to consider how elasticity might vary over time. More use of the extract is required. The last paragraph suggests that more substitutes are being developed along with new technology, which could make oil less price inelastic over time as substitutes emerge.

(d) An indirect tax on oil has the effect of shifting supply inwards from S_1 to S_2 on the diagram. **a** This includes both a specific tax (58 pence) and an *ad valorem* tax (23 pence) per litre. **b** Overall there is a pivotal shift in the supply curve. The new price is P_2 and output falls to Q_2. The tax area is shown by XYP_2W. The tax acts like an increase in production costs for firms and so they try and pass this on to consumers via higher prices. **c** Petrol companies may experience a drop in profits.

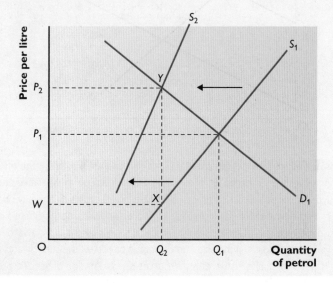

8/14 marks. a A correct diagram and its explanation are provided by the student (5 marks). **b** Application to the tax data in Figure 1 (1 mark) and suggesting **c** the tax is like a production cost, leading to lower profits, are also credited (1 + 1 marks). However, no evaluation marks are gained. Evaluation could include a discussion of petrol being an essential good and so the demand curve would be price inelastic and drawn to show this. Reference to the incidence of taxation between consumers and producers would also be useful — it is likely that consumers pay most of the tax. Discussion could include the impact on employment in the petrol market and the knock-on effects in other markets. The possibility of tax evasion and government failure are other ways to develop evaluative points. Overall the answer is too brief. This student receives 8/8 KAA marks and 0/6 evaluation marks.

(e) A subsidy is a government grant to firms to increase production. **a** The effects are shown in the diagram, where the supply curve shifts outwards from S to S_2. Output increases from Q_e to Q_2 and price falls from P_e to P_2. The total area of subsidy is $GLRP_2$. **b** The case for subsidising alternative energy sources is that it can help reduce air pollution associated with burning fossil fuels such as oil and coal. For example, by having electric powered cars it means cleaner air in towns and cities and so there should be a reduction in respiratory diseases and less pressure on healthcare resources. It can also help slow down climate change and the problem of poor crop harvests. In addition, these non-renewable energy sources can last longer for future generations to enjoy and assist with their economic growth. **c**

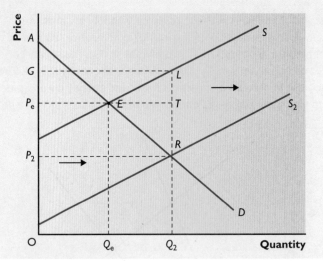

8/14 marks. a The student defines subsidy (1 mark) and then **b** explains the effect on output and price through a diagram (3 marks). **c** The benefits from developing alternative energy sources are explained, such as less pollution, less pressure on healthcare provision and a reduction in consumption of non-renewable energy (4 marks). However, no evaluation is offered — a common feature of this student's answers. Consequently, just the 8 KAA marks can be awarded. Evaluation marks could be gained by discussing the size and opportunity cost of the subsidy and the long time period involved in developing alternative energy sources. Consideration of specific problems with alternative energy sources would also help — this comes from extra reading. For example, electric powered vehicles have severe limits on the speed and distances they can travel. Furthermore, an infrastructure needs to be put in place, consisting of electricity charge points which need to be made available throughout the UK. There is also the problem that the electricity powering such motor vehicles could come from burning fossil fuels at power stations.

Total score: 28/48 = grade C

Question 3 **Road traffic growth**

Table 1 Transport statistics and average gross weekly income, 1998–2008 (Great Britain)

	1998	2003	2008	% rise 1998–2008
Licensed private cars (millions)	22.1	25.3	27.1	22.6%
Private cars (billion vehicle kilometres)	370.6	393.1	401.7	8.4%
Public roads in use (km)	389,000	392,000	395,000	1.6%
Average gross weekly household income (£ current prices)	£457	£571	£714	56.2%

Source: adapted from Annual Abstract of Statistics 2011

Table 2 The cost of travel by motor vehicle, rail and bus 1998–2008 (Great Britain)

	1998	2003	2008
Motoring (cars)	100	106.6	114.4
Bus fares	100	120.6	153.9
Rail fares	100	113.9	140.3
Retail price index	100	111.3	131.9

Source: Annual Abstract of Statistics 2011

Extract 1

Is road pricing the solution to road congestion?

People are more dependent on their cars than ever, driving further to work, schools and shops. This has contributed to a dramatic increase in road congestion. According to a government study, motorists waste up to 26 minutes for every 10 miles they travel on England's main roads, compared to journey times when traffic is flowing freely. The cost could total some £28 billion a year by 2025.

A nationwide system of road pricing might be the answer. A government report on transport recommended that motorists pay up to £1.30 per mile during peak times on major roads. The scheme would operate by installing satellite boxes in each vehicle, with varying charges set depending on the congestion and time of day. It would help reduce air and noise pollution and the funds raised could be re-invested into the transport infrastructure. It could also reduce non-essential car journeys and encourage more people to work from home whenever possible.

However, road pricing is very unpopular with motorists. In 2007, more than 1.8 million people signed a petition against a nationwide road congestion charge. Many see it as another opportunity for the government to tax motorists who already pay the highest fuel taxes in Europe. There are also implications for businesses such as road haulage firms, transporting goods, and motorists travelling to work. For many, bus and rail transport is not a realistic alternative to the motor car.

(a) **With reference to Tables 1 and 2, explain two likely reasons for the increase in the number of licensed private cars between 1998 and 2008.**

(6 marks)

e These questions offer marks for the explicit use of data in both tables, so make sure you refer to them in your answer.

(b) **Distinguish between the private costs and external costs of motoring.**

(4 marks)

e Always define key economic concepts in questions like this.

(c) **With reference to Table 1, discuss the likely effectiveness of building more roads as a means of reducing road congestion.**

(10 marks)

e Make use of the data in Table 1 as instructed and consider how the trends will shape your answer. Be prepared to calculate the percentage change in data to compare the trends – in this case it has already been provided in Table 1.

(d) **Referring to the extract and the concept of external costs, examine the case for a national road pricing scheme. Use an appropriate diagram to support your answer.**

(14 marks)

e This question offers an ideal opportunity to evaluate by considering the limitations of the case for a national road pricing scheme.

(e) **Discuss the reason why 'for many, bus and rail transport is not a realistic alternative to the motor car' (Extract 1).**

(14 marks)

e This question asks for a discussion and will require a conclusion at the end based on the relative merits of the points raised.

> **Student answer**
>
> **(a)** The first reason for the increase in the number of licensed private cars is due to a rise in the population. There has been an increase in immigration to the UK following the expansion of the European Union. This has enabled migrants to come to Britain to look for work. It is useful to have a car in order to become more mobile when looking for work. a The second reason is due to an increase in women in the workforce and so now there will be a greater demand for cars. b

Edexcel AS Economics

ⓔ **3/6 marks. a** The first reason has some development (2 marks). **b** The second reason is an identification point (1 mark). The student has not made use of the data available as instructed by the question. Consequently, a mark cap comes into force of a maximum of 4 marks. Reference should have been made to Table 1, which shows an increase in average gross weekly income of 56.2%, enabling people to afford to buy and run a car. It suggests that cars are a normal good with a positive income elasticity of demand. Reference should also be made to Table 2, which reveals the real cost of motoring to have fallen (since it has increased more slowly than the RPI), whereas the real cost of substitutes, such as bus and rail transport, has risen (since they have increased at a faster rate than the RPI).

> **(b)** Private costs are internal to an exchange which the price mechanism directly takes into account — for example, a motorist would have to pay for the car and fuel. External costs are negative third party effects which are outside the market transaction — for example, road congestion and air pollution caused by motor vehicles.

ⓔ **4/4 marks.** This is a much better answer where the student defines both concepts (1+1 marks) and offers relevant examples (1+1 marks)

> **(b)** Building more roads will not reduce traffic congestion since it cannot keep up with the growth in motor vehicles. The time taken to build roads also makes congestion worse in the short run as diversions appear and it could slow down the usual flow of traffic. It is also very expensive to build roads and the opportunity cost might involve forgoing an increase in government spending on healthcare and education. Alternatively, the government could reduce its borrowing if it stops building new roads. The government does not have the money to afford a major road building programme. Another reason why road building is not effective is because there is a shortage of land to build on especially in urban areas and the south-east of England. Building lots of new roads would have too great an environmental impact, causing massive external costs such as visual pollution and damage to wildlife **a**.
>
> However, if the road building focuses on areas which suffer from great traffic congestion, then it will have some positive effect. Main areas of road congestion include the M1 and M25 motorways. But then in the long run, it might increase the number of motorists using the roads until there is lots of congestion again. It is like an increase in supply leading to an increase in demand for a good **b**.

ⓔ **8/10 marks. a** The student develops several reasons why road building is not an effective means of reducing traffic congestion (cannot keep pace with growth in motor traffic, very expensive and a shortage of land) (4 marks). Usually, these points would easily be enough to secure all 6 KAA marks available but unfortunately there is no data reference from Table 1. For example, it shows that over the period the increase in private cars (22.6%) and billion vehicle kilometres travelled (8.4%) considerably outstripped the growth of roads in use (1.6%).**b** Good evaluation is offered which raises the possibility of selective road building schemes alleviating congestion though ultimately it is doomed by more motorists being encouraged to make use of the network (4 marks).

(c) There is a strong case for a national road pricing scheme. It will enable the government to increase the price of motoring for those who cause the congestion. The external costs can be greatly reduced by a road pricing scheme. It is a way of making the polluter pay for the congestion and so internalising the negative externalities. This is shown on the diagram where the road charge shifts the marginal private cost curve from MPC to MPC_1. It reduces the number of motor vehicle journeys from OQ_e to OQ_1 and increases the price per journey from OP_e to OP_1. The social optimum position is reached where marginal social costs equal marginal social benefits and the triangle of welfare loss XYW is eliminated. It seems fair that the motorists who cause the traffic congestion should pay for it by the road charge. I have assumed that there are no external benefits from motoring and so marginal private benefits equal marginal social benefits in the example. **a**

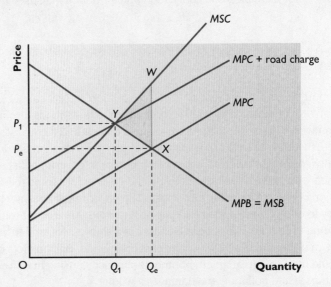

However, there are some problems associated with road pricing. These include the impact on low-income motorists who will find it difficult to use their cars. These people may seek to work closer to home and so reduce overall their geographical mobility of labour. There is also a danger that motorists use minor routes which are not subject to a road charge. It could mean greater congestion on these roads and more damage to their structure. Furthermore, it could reduce the amount of trade for businesses located along routes subject to high road tolls. **b**

🄔 **11/14 marks a** The answer provides a relevant diagram and explanation of how a road price scheme might internalise external costs (5 marks), but there is no use of ideas from the extract (for example, the monetary estimates of the cost of congestion and impact on air and noise pollution). **b** Three disadvantages of road pricing are developed and so six evaluation marks are gained (2 + 2 + 2 marks). However, the main drawback of the answer is a failure to use the extract information, which could have made it easier to secure the full marks.

(c) Bus and rail transport might not be a realistic alternative to the motor car since they are inconvenient to use. For example, they might be unreliable and so people end up late for work. The frequency of service is often quite limited and so creates inflexibility for workers and businesses relying upon them. Also, they involve journeys to and from stations and so represent extra hassle. Typically, bus journeys take much longer than car journeys. Then there is the issue of cleanliness and safety of travel. **a**

However, there are some advantages of public transport. People can often work on trains, making use of the journey time. Also there are no parking fees or problems in finding spaces to park. Motorists travelling into major conurbations may even face a congestion charge — for example, the London congestion charge. It could end up being cheaper to go by train than motor car. Trains also have faster journey times than cars over long distances. **b**

ⓔ 10/14 marks. a Several good points are mentioned which support the statement made (inconvenient, unreliable, frequency and time consuming) (6 marks). The answer could be strengthened by use of Table 2, which shows how bus and rail fares have risen at a faster rate than car journeys over the period 1998–2008, so there might be a financial reason why bus and train travel are unrealistic alternatives. Perhaps reference could be made to government spending cuts to reduce the fiscal deficit — the likelihood is that subsidies will be cut, worsening bus and rail services further. **b** Some evaluation is offered by suggesting that bus and rail travel may have several advantages over car travel, especially on longer journeys (4 marks). The answer could be improved by referring to economic concepts such as cross elasticity of demand and the extent to which motor vehicles and bus and rail travel are substitutes for each other. This will depend upon the individual's journey and so might range from zero to above +1.

Total score 36/48 = grade B

Question 4 **UK healthcare provision**

Table 1 Number of NHS staff by occupation, 1997–2010

Occupation	1997	2010	% increase
Doctors and consultants	89,619	141,326	57.7
Nurses	318,856	410,615	28.8
Scientific and technical staff	96,298	151,607	57.4
Managers	22,173	40,094	80.8
Other support staff	531,740	442,929	−16.7
Total	**1,058,686**	**1,186,571**	**12.0**

Sources: The King's Fund and ONS, 2011

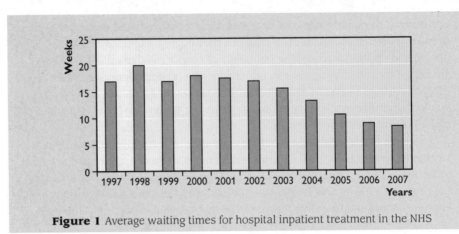

Figure 1 Average waiting times for hospital inpatient treatment in the NHS

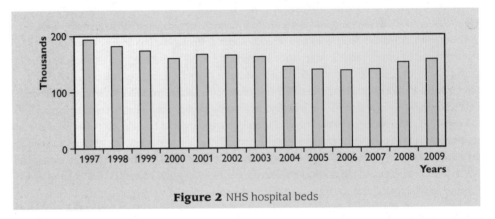

Figure 2 NHS hospital beds

Extract 1

Growing pressures on the NHS

The NHS is the largest employer in Europe. It treats over 1 million patients every 36 hours. Between 1997 and 2011 government spending on the NHS increased in real terms from £58 billion to £126 billion. It now comprises 8.4% of GDP, but this is still below the EU average of 9.3%.

The increase in NHS spending reflects rising demand and cost pressures: for example, changes in the size and age structure of the population and public expectations over standards. Over 100 new hospitals have been built since 1997 along with employment of extra staff.

However, not all the money seems to have been well spent. Staff salaries have soared and account for 40% of the NHS budget, while productivity has fallen by 0.4% a year since 1997. On the other hand, this fall in productivity is disputed by staff, who point to improvements in the quality of treatment and better job satisfaction.

The NHS provides free healthcare at the point of consumption. However, this has created an excess demand for treatment, leading to long waiting lists. As the government focuses on reducing its budget deficit, average waiting times and the number of people waiting for treatment are likely to increase.

(a) Explain two likely causes of the increase in government spending on the NHS over the period referred to in Extract 1. **(6 marks)**

e Make sure you use the pointers from the extract and try to develop them further.

(b) Using examples, explain the relevance of 'opportunity cost' to the increase in government spending on the NHS. **(4 marks)**

e Always define the key concept in the question and give examples.

(c) To what extent has 'free healthcare at the point of consumption' created an excess demand for treatment in the NHS? Use a supply and demand diagram in your answer. **(10 marks)**

e You should consider the degree to which you agree with the statement, supporting your argument with evidence. Your evaluation could include a discussion of why healthcare is provided free or the implications of introducing fees. Be prepared to offer up to two evaluation points for 10 mark-base questions.

(d) Assess the importance of private and external benefits arising from the consumption of healthcare. Illustrate your answer with an appropriate diagram. **(14 marks)**

e The command word 'assess' invites you to estimate the quality or quantity of something. In the case of externalities, you can raise the difficulty of measuring them. Be prepared to offer up to three evaluation points for 14 mark-base questions.

(e) Discuss whether increased funding of the NHS has improved the quality of healthcare provision. **(14 marks)**

e Discussion can include both positive and negative effects of increased healthcare funding and a conclusion is required. Be prepared to offer up to three evaluation points for 14 mark-base questions.

Student answer

(a) The increase in government spending could be due to 'demand pressures' from population changes in the UK. There is an ageing population which means that as people get older they are more prone to illness and so make greater use of doctors and hospitals. There has also been an increase in the population over recent years due to immigration from central and eastern Europe. **a** A second cause could be due to 'cost pressures' from an increase in the supply of factor inputs — for example, 100 new hospitals and many more doctors and nurses employed. All this costs money which has to be paid for by the government through increasing taxes. **b**

e **6/6 marks.** The student has made effective use of the prompts in the extract and developed them further to achieve full marks. **a** The first point considers demand pressures from a growing and ageing population (3 marks). **b** The second point considers the costs associated with supply: namely, more hospitals and staffing (3 marks).

(b) Opportunity cost refers to the value of the next best alternative forgone. **a** The rise in government spending on the NHS from £58 billion to £126 billion **b** has an opportunity cost since the funds could have been spent on education or defence instead. Alternatively, the government could have reduced the size of the fiscal deficit which appears to be a key priority today. **c**

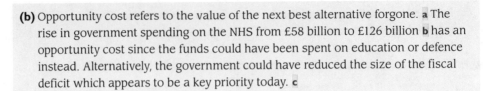 **4/4 marks. a** Definition of opportunity cost (1 mark). **b** Use of figures to show increase in government spending on NHS (1 mark). **c** Examples of alternative use of the funds provided (2 marks).

(c) Free healthcare at the point of use has created an excess demand. **a** This is where demand exceeds supply at the set price, in this case zero. This is shown in the diagram as the quantity Q_eQ_2. Supply of healthcare is a vertical line to represent the fixed budget for the NHS. **b**

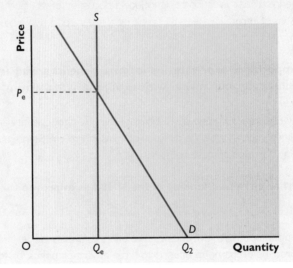

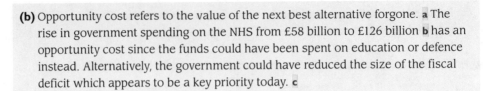 **4/10 marks. a** The explanation of the cause of excess demand is correct but too brief (2 marks). One might explain that people may seek treatment for very minor ailments since there is no financial incentive to deter this. **b** The diagram is drawn accurately and excess demand is identified (2 marks). Reference could also be made to the idea that a free market in healthcare would eliminate the excess demand by allowing price to rise to OP_e and quantity to fall to OQ_e. Some evaluation is required to achieve the 4 marks available: for example, discussion of the magnitude of the excess demand or price elasticity of demand (which is likely to be inelastic). The student could make reference to Figure 1 which shows a fall in the average waiting time for treatment, implying a reduction in excess demand. Another valid comment is to distinguish between a 'want' and 'effective demand'. A free market in healthcare may eliminate excess demand, but many people go without treatment since they cannot afford to pay. The price mechanism simply ignores these people.

(d) Private benefits refer to the benefits internal to an exchange. **a** They include the benefits in terms of salaries to staff employed and the revenues gained by firms supplying healthcare services — for example, medicines and X-ray scanning equipment. Private benefits from healthcare are very important to the economy since it is a direct source of income and employment to thousands of people. **b** External benefits refer to third party benefits outside of a market transaction. **c** They include a healthier workforce, which means people take less time off work for illness and so are more productive. Furthermore, the government may experience improved finances since tax revenue should rise and spending on unemployment and disability benefits should fall. There is also a reduction in the spread of contagious diseases, since most people receive free vaccinations. This should increase the life expectancy of the general population and raise the supply of labour available for firms. **d**

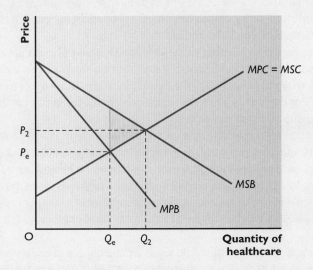

The diagram shows private, external and social benefits. It also reveals the area of welfare gain if healthcare provision is raised to the social optimum position of Q_2, where $MSB = MSC$. If left to the market, MSB would exceed MSC at output Q_e and so it is not the best position for society. **e** It appears that the external benefits to be gained are so important as to make it worthwhile for the government to spend £126 billion and fund this through taxation rather than leave it to the private sector. The shaded triangle represents the area of welfare gain where social benefits exceed social costs for the output slice Q_eQ_2. **f**

ⓔ 12/14 marks. a Definition of private benefits (1 mark). **b** Application of types of private benefits to healthcare (2 marks). **c** Definition of external benefits (1 mark). **d** Application of types of external benefits to healthcare (2 marks). **e** Diagram with explanation (5 marks). However, a maximum of 8 KAA marks is available here. **f** Two evaluative comments are made by suggesting that the external benefits gained are important enough for the government to fund through taxation and by discussion of the area of welfare gain (2 + 2 marks). Another way to evaluate would be to include discussion of the difficulty of quantifying and then attaching a monetary value

to external benefits from healthcare — it is difficult to place a value on the benefit from reducing the spread of contagious diseases.

(e) Increased funding of the NHS has definitely improved the quality of healthcare. The magnitude of the real increase in spending (117%) has ensured this. Table 1 shows a 57.7% increase in the number of doctors and a 28.8% increase in nurses. This probably helped to reduce average waiting times shown in Figure 1 from around 17 weeks in 1997 to 8 weeks by 2007. **a**

However, Figure 2 shows that the number of hospital beds has fallen from nearly 200,000 to around 160,000 over the period. This suggests the quantity of healthcare has reduced. Yet we are told that the NHS treats more than 1 million people every 36 hours. It could be that advances in treatment mean patients do not have to spend so long in hospital and so fewer beds are required. Perhaps focus should be on the type of hospital beds available — whether general or specialist beds, since the latter are linked to intensive care and we do not want these to be in short supply. Moreover, there has been an increase in the number of hospital beds between 2006 and 2009.

To make a better evaluation we need to know what the extra government funding has been spent on. If most of it has been on staff salaries then the quality of provision may not be so good. The extract indicates that 40% of the NHS budget is spent on staff salaries. Yet significant increases in pay can help boost staff morale and increase productivity.

Table 1 shows a bigger rate of increase in the employment of health managers than doctors and nurses, which some people might suggest is a waste of money and does not help patient care. However, the size of the healthcare budget is so massive that lots of managers are needed to allocate funds properly. It could lead to a more efficient use of resources. Also the number of managers appears to be quite small (40,000) when compared to the total number employed in the NHS (1,180,000).

Furthermore, it is very difficult to measure the quality of healthcare provision. For example, the decrease in productivity could simply mean more time and care is being spent treating each patient. The quality of healthcare may have improved. We need further information on things like success rates from different treatments and perhaps results from surveys on customer satisfaction. **b**

ⓔ **14/14 marks.** The student makes effective use of the data and integrates the analysis and evaluation together. This is a good way of answering the larger mark-base questions. **a** The data are used to directly answer the question (2 marks). **b** The next four paragraphs reveal an informed critical approach to extra government spending on healthcare, which means that all the KAA and evaluation marks are achieved through presenting balanced arguments (3 + 3 + 3 + 3 marks).

Total score: 40/48 = grade A

Knowledge check answers

1 The opportunity cost of you staying on at school to take A-levels is the next best alternative: for example, earning income from a job or joining an apprenticeship scheme to learn a trade.

2 Opportunity cost can be shown by a movement along a production possibility frontier: for example, from position A to B. An extra 10 units of manufactured goods are obtained at the expense of 5 units of services.

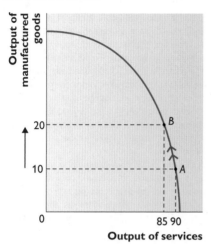

3 There must be unemployed resources in the economy — spare capacity exists.

4 An outward shift of the production possibility frontier might be caused by an increase in the quality or quantity of labour, an increase in capital goods (investment), new technology, enterprise and discovery of natural resources.

5 The division of labour means workers become more skilled at what they do through experience and repetition of tasks. It thereby leads to greater output.

6 The UK is a mixed economy since both private enterprise and the government decide how resources are allocated for production and distribution.

7 As the price of a good falls it becomes more affordable for consumers to buy with their income. Also, it becomes relatively cheaper than substitute goods and so some consumers will switch to buying it.

8 A change in the price of the good in question. A rise in price will lead to a contraction in demand and a fall in price will lead to an extension in demand.

9 The main factors include a change in price of substitute or complementary goods and a change in income or tastes. Note that changes in the price of the good will not shift the demand curve.

10 The minus sign means there is an inverse relationship between the change in price and the change in demand. Thus, a rise in price will cause a fall in quantity demanded. The demand curve has a negative gradient.

11 The answer indicates how much a 1% change in price causes demand to change by. For example, an answer of 3 means that a 1% change in price will lead to a 3% change in demand for the good.

12 If a firm knows the price elasticity of demand for the good it produces then it may be able to increase total revenue by changing the price. If demand is inelastic, a rise in price will increase total revenue; if demand is elastic, a fall in price will increase total revenue.

13 If the government knows the price elasticity of demand for a particular good then it will have an idea of the impact that an indirect tax will have on it. For example, a tax placed on a good with inelastic demand should lead to a high tax yield and have relatively little impact on demand.

14 Normal goods have a positive income elasticity of demand; as real income rises, demand for the good also rises. Inferior goods have a negative income elasticity of demand; as real income rises, demand for the good falls.

15 Complementary goods have a negative cross elasticity of demand: for example, a fall in price of computer games consoles will cause an increase in demand for computer games software. Substitute goods have a positive cross elasticity of demand: for example, a rise in price of beef may cause an increase in demand for lamb.

16 As the price of a good rises, there is an incentive to supply more since the firm might achieve higher profits. It is also able to cover the extra costs involved in producing more of the good.

17 A change in the price of the good in question. A rise in price will lead to an extension in supply and a fall in price will lead to a contraction in supply.

18 The main factors include a change in costs of production, technology, the ability of firms to enter and exit an industry, indirect taxes and government subsidies. Note that changes in the price of the good will not shift the supply curve.

19 A positive number means there is a direct relationship between the change in price and the change in quantity supply. Thus, a rise in price will cause a rise in the quantity supplied. The supply curve has a positive gradient.

20 The figure indicates by how much a 1% change in price causes quantity supplied to change. For example, an answer of 2 means that a 1% change in price will lead to a 2% change in quantity supplied of the good.

21 For most goods, supply tends to be relatively price inelastic in the short run as some factor inputs are fixed in quantity, but becomes relatively price elastic in the long run when all factor inputs are variable.

22 If supply exceeds demand, price will fall, leading to an extension in demand and a contraction in supply. Eventually, equilibrium position is reached.

23 If demand exceeds supply, price will rise, leading to an extension in supply and contraction in demand. Eventually, equilibrium position is reached.

24 An increase in supply of a good will cause its price to fall and so increase consumer surplus.

25 A decrease in demand for a good will cause its price to fall and so lead to a decrease in producer surplus.

26 A specific tax is placed as a fixed amount per unit of good and causes an inward parallel shift in the supply curve. An *ad valorem* tax is placed as a percentage of the price of a good and causes an inward pivotal shift in the supply curve.

27 A unit subsidy will shift the supply curve outwards (an increase in supply) and reduce the equilibrium price.

28 Derived demand refers to the demand for a factor input (such as labour) being dependent upon the demand for the final product it makes. For example, the demand for motor vehicle workers depends on the demand for the motor vehicles they make.

29 An NMW set below the market equilibrium wage will have no effect. The NMW is a legal minimum wage and so wage rates can be any level above this.

30 Social costs are the total of private costs and external costs.

31 Social benefits are the total of private benefits and external benefits.

32 Market equilibrium is the output position where marginal private benefits (*MPB*) equal marginal private costs (*MPC*). Externalities are ignored. However, the social optimum is where marginal social benefits (*MSB*) equal marginal social costs (*MSC*).

33 The welfare loss triangle is the area on an externality diagram that depicts the excess of social costs over social benefits for a given level of output.

34 The welfare gain triangle is the area on an externality diagram that depicts the excess of social benefits over social costs for a given output level.

35 Public goods are defined by their characteristics of non-excludability and non-rivalry in the provision of a good.

36 Public goods are a type of market failure since there would be no provision or very little provision of them in a free market. This is due to the free rider problem — where it is possible to consume the goods without paying for them. Consequently, there is no profit incentive for firms to provide them.

37 Imperfect market knowledge leads to market failure because individuals and firms may make decisions on buying or selling a good which reduces their overall welfare.

38 The immobility of labour leads to market failure because workers may be unable to take available job vacancies due to geographical or occupational barriers. It means that some labour resources are inefficiently allocated to a particular job or not in employment at all.

39 Demand for agricultural goods tends to be price inelastic and so a good harvest (increase in supply) will reduce total revenue and a poor harvest (decrease in supply) will raise total revenue.

40 High taxes are placed on tobacco, alcohol and petrol in order to internalise external costs. They are a way of making the polluters pay for these costs. In addition, they provide significant tax revenue to the government since demand is typically price inelastic for these goods.

41 The government typically subsidises goods which have significant external benefits in production or consumption: for example, renewable energy sources, public transport and healthcare.

42 A 'cap and trade' scheme is where the government limits the amount of pollution that firms are able to emit but also allows them to buy and sell pollution permits between themselves.

43 Property rights refer to an organisation being given legal responsibility for the management and control of a particular resource, determining what it can be used for and by whom.

44 The absence of property rights may lead to the exploitation of resources such as the seas: for example, dumping toxic waste or over-fishing with the result that fish stocks are depleted for future generations.

45 The purpose of a buffer stock scheme is to reduce price fluctuations and stabilise producer incomes. It is also an attempt to ensure supplies of a good for consumers.

46 An agency buys in times of a good harvest and releases from its stockpile in times of a bad harvest in order to maintain the target price.